# WORD ON THE STREET

"*Engagement That Rocks* isn't just a management business book; it's a cultural anthem. I have seen firsthand the power of an engaged workforce, and Jim Knight has given us the perfect blueprint to make that happen. Blending rock star storytelling with real-world tactics that actually get people tuned in and turned on, this employee-oriented set list is designed to take the business to legendary heights."

**Kelli Valade**, CEO, Denny's

"In a world of digital interfaces and endless choices, it's the human touches that define hospitality. *Engagement That Rocks* is a call to lead with empathy, inspire from the inside and scale culture like sound waves. For any brand hoping to make guests feel seen, known and remembered—this book is your set list."

**Noah Glass**, founder and CEO, Olo

"*Engagement That Rocks* is like getting a cultural tune-up—from the inside out. Jim Knight brings decades of insight on employee engagement and packages it in a way that hits hard and sticks. If you want your people to go from rented interest to real commitment, start with this book."

**Joseph Sheetz**, chairman of the board, Sheetz

"Jim Knight's *Engagement That Rocks* is a true love letter to leadership in today's fast-paced world. With his rock and roll background and leadership expertise, Jim brings a fresh and engaging perspective on how to create a culture that not only retains top talent but makes them fall in love with their workplace. It's an engaging and insightful read that every leader should have on their shelf."

**Clint Pulver**, Emmy Award winner, employee retention expert and author of *I Love It Here*

"Jim Knight has written the kind of book that every person that is put in a leadership position with a pulse—and a responsibility to people—needs to read right now. *Engagement That Rocks* doesn't just talk about employee engagement; it lives it. From the first page, Jim brings a jolt of realness, experience and humanity to a topic too often reduced to corporate buzzwords. This is your backstage pass to creating a place where people want to show up, plug in and give it everything they've got."

**John Manes**, chairman of the board, StorSuite

"Reading this book felt like getting front row seats to the greatest gig in company culture. Jim Knight isn't just talking about engagement—he's living it, breathing it, and handing you the set list. This isn't HR fluff—it's a wake-up call to lead with heart, ditch the boring basics and create a workplace people never want to leave. It's fierce, fun and full of truth. Bravo, rock star."

**Melissa M. Wiggins**, Scottish firecracker, keynote speaker and author of *UnFollow*

"Hiring great people is one thing, but keeping them engaged is another. Jim Knight is a master storyteller, teacher and leadership coach. This might be the best employee engagement guide that I've ever read. If you care about the people you love and serve, read this book."

**Tommy Spaulding**, *New York Times* bestselling author of *The Heart-Led Leader* and *The Gift of Influence*

"Employee engagement remains a big challenge and high priority in most businesses today. In his book *Engagement That Rocks*, Jim Knight digs into this subject with clear understandings, tools and solutions that can change your business and its trajectory. Leaders should highly consider making this book a part of their set list!"

**Billy Downs**, president, Ford's Garage

"I met Jim Knight right after he wrote *Culture That Rocks*, and he blew me away with the notion that every company is one big band and the key to success is getting the band to play together in harmony. In *Engagement That Rocks*, Jim takes this concept a step further. Even more important than playing together is wanting, thriving and loving to play together—as a team, as a department, as a company. Jim tackles engagement the only way he knows how: with the energy of a rock-and-roll star and a pulse on employee loyalty amplified to the extreme. This book is a highly fun, energetic and addictive read."

**Josh Halpern**, CEO, Big Chicken

"You want to know how and why team engagement will enhance your organization at every level? You want over a hundred novel engagement ideas by real companies—big and small—that you can cherry pick and implement into your team? You want a candid conversation with one of the best executive-level trainers of the 21st century? You want more rock and roll metaphors than you thought existed? You got it all here with *Engagement That Rocks*. Bring your highlighter—you're going to need it."

**Dave Place**, owner and CEO, BizLadder

# ENGAGEMENT THAT ROCKS

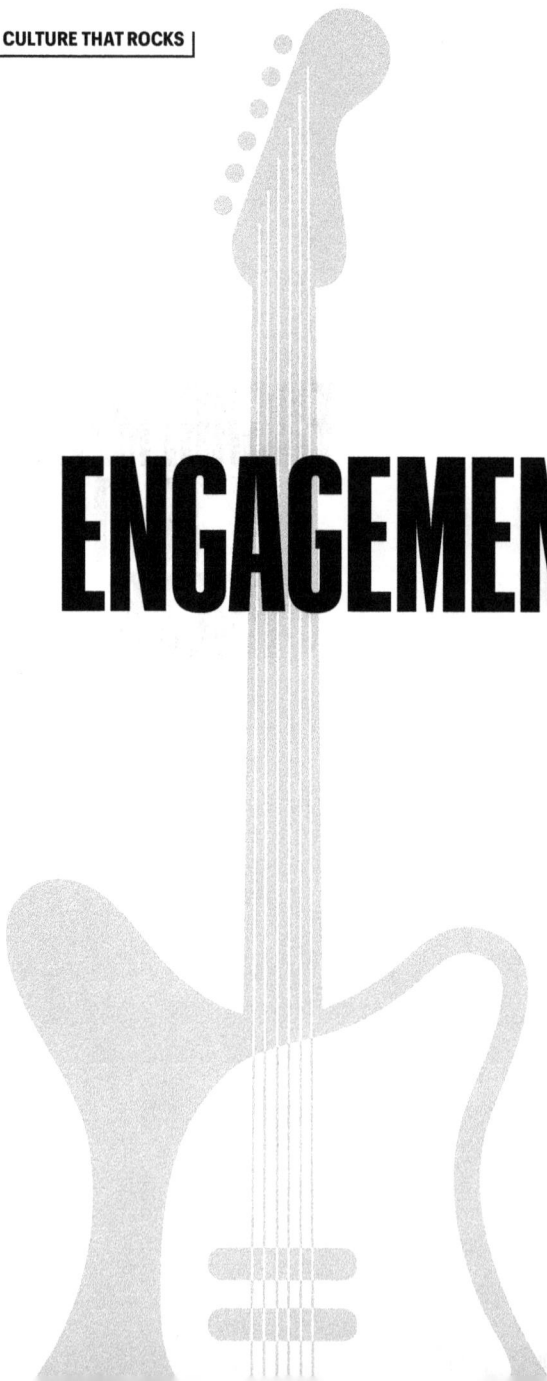

# ENGAGEMENT

# JIM KNIGHT

## ENHANCE EMPLOYEE EXPERIENCES AND RETAIN CHART-TOPPING TALENT

# THAT ROCKS

**PAGE TWO**

Cataloguing in publication information is
available from Library and Archives Canada.
ISBN 978-1-77458-512-2 (paperback)
ISBN 978-1-77458-513-9 (ebook)

Page Two
pagetwo.com

Page Two™ is a trademark owned by Page Two
Strategies Inc., and is used under license by
authorized licensees

Cover and interior design by Peter Cocking


knightspeaker.com

*For Madison—*

*whose superpower is*

*to light up the world.*

# SET LIST

# SOUND
## CHECK

APRIL 16, 1991.

I was in awe—mouth open, eyes bugged, mind racing and heart pounding.

Across from me was a restaurant manager with hair below his shoulders who delivered the company information with his sunglasses on the entire time. For three hours.

*That* was different.

But it elicited several questions. Was he trying to be cool? Was he exhausted? Or was he high? Maybe a little bit of each. But it was *definitely* different.

Beside me hung Eddie Van Halen's famous red-and-white-striped "Frankenstein" guitar, close enough for me to touch. Ninety decibels of Zeppelin were ringing in my ears. Buzzing about was without a doubt the most interesting collection of humans I'd ever seen in one place—every one of them moving at blazing speed, and with passion and intention.

The place was a sensory mosh-pit. It was a rush. And I was immediately hooked. If rock and roll were a tangible thing, this is what I imagined it would look and feel like. The energy, the intensity, the attitude, the diversity... wow! What a culture!

As the manager wove through the unbelievable story of the Hard Rock Cafe brand during my Day 1 Orientation, he turned his attention to the amazing benefits of joining the band:

- **Aesthetics**—Although there were strict standards in place, you could look however you wanted: tattoos, facial hair, long hair, colored hair, mohawks, multiple body piercings. As long as there was a "plan," you could freely express your individuality.

- **Free food**—Provided as a group meal at the start of every shift (or 50 percent off the menu). Believe me, this is a huge benefit for young adults. Ah, the power of free food.

- **Premium insurance**—Fantastic health and dental coverage was available at an inexpensive cost (free for managers), including low-cost vision insurance, which many employees took advantage of during the Lasik eye surgery boom in the 90s.

- **Retirement plan**—I'm so thankful that someone convinced me to allocate a portion of my bi-weekly pay to a 401(k) plan, starting on my first day...

since after 21 years, I was able to create a massive nest egg when I ultimately "retired" from the brand.

- **Christmas bonus**—The company doled out $100 for every year of service at the end of the year. For a host, busser or dishwasher, this was a sweet reward (and a real need for some) during the holidays.

- **Milestone awards**—Every employee, regardless of position, who reached ten years of full-time work received a custom Rolex watch. At 20 years, diamond upgrades were made to the face of the watch. These were real Rolexes, too. Of course, it helped that the brand bought them in bulk to bring the system-wide price down, but still … a Rolex!

- **Employee assistance fund**—Completely supported by cafe peers for those Rockers-in-need, voluntary contributions funded everything from weekly baby formula to monthly car payments to replacing houses that had burned to the ground from a lightning strike.

- **Global openings**—Employees who became trainers would immediately be eligible to train frontline new hires and travel to open new cafes in countries around the world.

- **Disability-favored**—The company attracted and hired people with disabilities; during my time with the brand in the early 90s, we had a deaf busser, a phone host who was in a wheelchair and a 4-foot-tall little person as a host trainer.

- **Internal promotions**—The company proudly advertised that their internal promotion rate into management was 90 percent versus hiring leaders from the outside. There were growth opportunities everywhere for those who wanted them.

- **Leadership support**—Although the only mention of this benefit in the orientation was of an "open door" policy and that managers would always "have your back," what I found over the years was a group of leaders who constantly taught, recognized and inspired everyone within their orbit. Bosses who actually cared about me as a whole person mattered.

At the time, this was the busiest restaurant in the world. And as spectacular as the benefits sounded as the facilitator revealed each, my mind kept reveling in the overall environment I then shared with several new Hard Rockers in that onboarding session: I was thrilled to now be working in a high-volume, fast-paced environment, ensconced in rock and roll music, surrounded by competent and cool people who accepted me for who I was. It was truly a dream job.

What started out as a summer gig for me eventually turned into a 21-year relationship with a single company—and unquestionably the career of a lifetime. A career that hailed from "joining the band" as a staff-level host and evolved through various management positions and corporate training levels, until I ultimately landed my final role as an executive with one of the most recognized and respected brands in the world. Sometimes, I get giddy thinking about the magnitude of my transition, from being unsure if I could even "hang with the band" to eventually reaching a level of responsibility that allowed me to affect and protect that iconic culture.

That job-of-a-lifetime absolutely rocked my world. And I could not wait to get to work every day. So, I'm curious...

- Have you ever worked for a company that got you *that* excited about showing up?

- Do you think your employees feel like that about your organization?

To be clear, although I have dedicated stories throughout the book listing tangible employee benefits—including an entire chapter that invites you to consider implementing some unique initiatives— my approach in writing *Engagement That Rocks* was to transcend simply providing a list of benefits as the way to attract and keep top talent. Retaining "rock stars" goes way beyond that. And most companies would not be able to afford many of the listed suggestions anyway.

That's where disciplined, ongoing and, many times, free employee engagement comes in.

Some of the initiatives Hard Rock employed were obviously quite expensive, but many cost nothing. It was an overarching philosophy the leaders had: to create such an unbelievable internal culture that employees would fall madly in love with the brand. And it worked. Nobody wanted to leave, and employees passed that love affair on to the guests. Ask yourself...

- As a leader, what little-to-no-cost initiatives could you immediately implement to keep team members fully engaged so they stick around and regularly deliver memorable experiences for customers?

- As a potential employee, what are the non-negotiable characteristics in a business that would influence your decision to join a company and that would keep you motivated?

If you are on a quest to strengthen your company's internal culture, this book is your blueprint. Amping up employee engagement is one of the greatest accelerants to lighting up a culture that rocks. Customers may not see the internal activities you plan to unleash among the staff, but they will absolutely be the ultimate recipients of that work.

In *Engagement That Rocks*, we will explore the various aspects of employee engagement, including its definition, drivers and benefits. I will also discuss the role of leadership and communication in promoting employee engagement... especially in today's attention-starved world. Finally, I will provide practical tips and strategies that any organization can use to enhance employee experiences and retain their best talent.

Whether you are a business leader, middle manager or HR professional, this book will provide you with the tools and knowledge you need to create a workplace culture that fosters employee engagement and drives organizational success.

Let's rock.

I don't treat the band like I'm above them ... I'd be very uncomfortable having to do this alone.

**TOM PETTY**

# SET
# THE STAGE

I N TODAY'S rapidly changing business environment, employee engagement has emerged as a critical factor in determining an organization's success. The term "employee engagement" refers to the entirety of the emotional, psychological and behavioral connection that employees have with their workplace. It's the extent to which staff members are committed to the goals of their organization and are motivated to contribute to its success.

In other words, it's the entire journey an employee takes with your organization.

According to Gallup's *State of the Global Workforce* report from January 1, 2023, only 15 percent of employees are fully engaged at work. That's a whopping 85 percent that are *not* engaged ... the largest disparity in history. Those 85 out of 100 employees are miserable at work, spread negativity to their colleagues, are surely exploring other jobs and are most likely to leave in the next 12 months.

This is not sustainable for any business.

## THE UNDENIABLE BENEFITS

Countless studies have shown that *engaged* employees are more productive, have higher job satisfaction and are more likely to stay with their employer. In contrast, *disengaged* employees are less productive, less motivated and more likely to leave their job at the first opportunity.

To set the stage, here are the top ten widely known, undeniable benefits of enhancing employee engagement:

1 **Improved employee satisfaction**—Engaged employees are happier with their jobs and enjoy going to work.

2 **Greater employee retention**—Engaged employees are more likely to stay with the company, reducing the cost and time associated with recruiting and training new employees.

3 **Improved employee well-being**—Engaged employees have a positive work-life balance, leading to better physical and mental health.

4 **Increased innovation**—Engaged employees are more creative, leading to new ideas and solutions for the company.

5 **Better teamwork**—Engaged employees are more likely to work well together, leading to improved collaboration and solutions.

6 **Heightened employee morale**—Engaged employees are more positive, leading to a more enjoyable work environment.

7 **Increased productivity**—Engaged employees are more motivated and focused, leading to better overall results for the company.

8 **Better customer satisfaction**—Engaged employees are more likely to provide excellent customer service, leading to increased brand loyalty.

9 **Higher profits**—Engaged employees are more likely to be productive and efficient, leading to increased financial results for the company.

10 **Enhanced brand reputation**—A company with engaged employees is viewed as a positive, reputable place to work, which can help attract top talent and customer loyalty.

If these proven outcomes of having engaged employees don't motivate you to seriously and immediately re-evaluate your practices for internal team members,

I don't know what will. As you can see, *everyone* wins with a highly engaged workforce. Organizations that want to remain competitive in the war for talent *must* find ways to enhance the employee experience and foster a positive work environment.

## MY UNIQUE PERSPECTIVE

When it comes to the topic of employee engagement, I have a lot to share. My opinions are not unique to HR professionals who focus on this concept daily or rock star brands who already enjoy the fruits of their businesses' successes. However, I *am* hypersensitive to what employee engagement *could be* because of the two decades I spent working in human resources for one of the greatest employee-oriented companies on the planet: Hard Rock International. No doubt, the time I spent immersed in that authentic, unpredictable and sometimes irreverent hospitality brand shaped who I am today and my philosophies, but those years were just the catalyst for the employee engagement concepts I now share with companies around the world.

The Clash's Joe Strummer famously said, "Without people you're nothing." Meaning, behind every thriving band are the teammates that make it happen. That mindset was embedded in Hard Rock's DNA at its inception and became a guiding principle for how I believe every leader should approach their people— investing in them not just as workers but as partners in the brand's success.

Since I "retired" from corporate life, I've had the great fortune to give keynote speeches to fantastic organizations in many different industries and countries, I've studied and spent time with amazing leaders who have taken their brands to iconic heights, and I've written bestselling books on the topics of company culture, leadership and customer service. This book is the next evolution, designed to help companies internally differentiate themselves from their competitors to achieve long-term sustainability and relevance.

## THE SERIES

When I launched my book *Culture That Rocks* in 2014, I laid out a holistic approach to enhancing a company, which touched on many facets of organizational culture. The concepts were solid, but some areas screamed for further exploration and more detail. This

# HIGHLY ENGAGED EMPLOYEES CAN'T FATHOM NOT WORKING FOR THE BRAND.

———

was the rationale for the "Culture That Rocks" series. The plan was to deconstruct my first "book baby" into three specific, detailed and relevant books, each with its own heightened message and set of learnings.

*Leadership That Rocks* was the series's first book, which focused on helping new, up-and-coming and middle managers in creating, maintaining or revolutionizing a company's culture. *Service That Rocks* came next, highlighting how critical the customer experience is in delivering a brand's sustained success. Now, I present the final book in the series, *Engagement That Rocks*—the book you are reading now—which puts a spotlight on enhancing employee experiences, thereby developing a vibrant internal culture.

Like those that came before it, this book includes ideas, stories and best practices for how to strengthen the internal culture of a business. *Engagement That Rocks: Enhance Employee Experiences and Retain Chart-Topping Talent* is the final act in the three-book series and focuses on creating such a fantastic working environment for employees that they cannot fathom *not* working for the brand.

Here are the other books in this "Culture That Rocks" series:

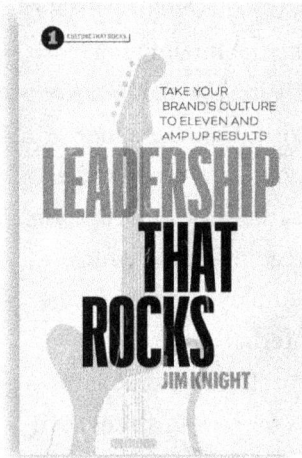

**LEADERSHIP
THAT ROCKS**
Take Your Brand's
Culture to Eleven and
Amp Up Results
2021

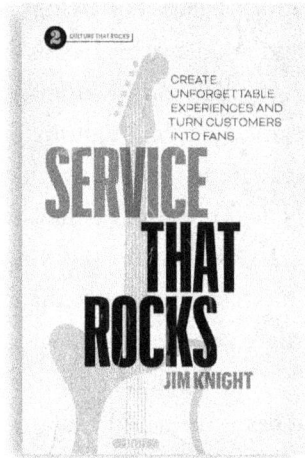

**SERVICE
THAT ROCKS**
Create Unforgettable
Experiences and Turn
Customers into Fans
2022

Each book stands alone as a targeted and robust resource that addresses a specific need of the business—and that may be the exact solution your company needs to amp up results. But if you collect the entire series, you will be investing in a detailed and holistic blueprint for sustaining your company's culture at legendary heights.

And *that* will get you to rock icon status that much faster.

## THE REAL WORK

The real impact will come when you put in the work of studying and implementing my suggestions. I'm an educator at heart; my hope is that you actively apply the ideas I share with you so that you create a best-in-class employee culture.

At the end of each chapter, I provide an at-a-glance review of its most impactful points. Consider these the main lyrics of the overall tune, so that you don't get lost in the melody and the beat. Do yourself a favor: Don't skip over the chapter endings. In addition to this low-hanging fruit, the "Encore" section at the end of the book includes action items you can do to immediately enhance your employee engagement and ignite your brand's cultural revolution from the inside.

*Engagement That Rocks* could be just an interesting read for some—which is cool—but for those serious about solidifying their brand's legacy, amping up the internal company culture is the best and most sustainable way to do this.

# #1 GREATEST HIT

1 **Employee engagement isn't a nice-to-have perk**—It's a critical part of a company's culture. You can't build a legendary brand without engaged people.

You're only as good
as the people you
surround yourself with.

**KEITH RICHARDS
(THE ROLLING STONES)**

# IMPLEMENT AN EMPLOYEE-FIRST PHILOSOPHY

**N**OW THAT we live in a post-pandemic world, the need for employee engagement has never been more crucial. Starting in 2019, the entire business community went through a shared global experience: Among many other struggles, we all navigated the challenges of remote work. Having to adapt to a distance-based landscape, where connection goes beyond office walls and into their homes, team members had a spotlight on them like never before. And business changed forever.

Most company leaders now realize that employee engagement, perhaps more than the work process itself or the overall company productivity, is the glue that keeps our professional bonds strong... even from a distance. The environment today demands more than just employees clocking in and out; it calls for something bigger than a job—more than a means to an end. As Steven Van Zandt of the E Street Band once said, "Bands are like families, and if you don't take care of your family, it falls apart." The same goes for the workplace—if leaders neglect the people who make the music of the business, the harmony quickly fades.

Humans need connection. Employees need engagement. Leaders need awareness. So, where do we start?

We hyper-focus on the employee, *not* the end user of our products and services. We make mission #1 about the team members. Catering to today's workforce is the backstage pass to success.

But here's the kicker: Not all engagement strategies are created equal; you can't cater to everyone the same way. Today's team members are a diverse ensemble, each with unique needs, challenges and aspirations. As a leader, your job is to tune into their frequency, understand their needs and create an environment where every individual can shine.

## PRICE OF ADMISSION VERSUS AMPLIFIERS

Sadly, many companies focus on the basic "price of admission"—the bare minimum to keep employees from disengaging—like pay and benefits. However, you're not here for the basics, are you? You're here to turn up the volume on the employee experience

# CATERING TO TODAY'S WORKFORCE IS THE BACKSTAGE PASS TO SUCCESS.

———

so that your employees resonate with loyalty and dedication.

To do that, you'll need to focus on *amplifiers*—the innovative programs and approaches that rock star leaders use to retain chart-topping talent. These amplifiers are the secret sauce that creates an environment where employees don't just work; they become invested, loyal and driven to contribute their very best. They become brand ambassadors, even when they are not at work.

According to Gallup's 2024 *The State of American Workplace* report, an astounding 31 percent of employees left their last job in pursuit of a better work-life balance and personal well-being. That's one-third of the entire workforce! So, if you're not one of those favored landing spots, whose left making the donuts?

In a world where the lines between work life and personal life are blurred, the quest for balance and well-being has become a resounding anthem. The Gallup revelation underscores a crucial truth: Today's employees are not just seeking a job; they're on a mission to align their professional pursuits with personal fulfillment.

The traditional playbook, where profit and productivity led the charge, has evolved. Now, the spotlight is on prioritizing the well-being and work-life balance of those who make the workplace pulse with energy: the employees. Therefore, we need to flip the narrative. It's a call to action to place employees at the forefront of our strategies, decisions and culture. The rallying cry for engagement *should* be "Employees First." If you start with that mindset, your business will transcend ordinary and become extraordinary as you create an environment where employees don't just exist—they thrive.

## The Container Store

One company that exemplifies this approach is The Container Store. This product-based business has an "employee-first" philosophy that is the cornerstone of its ongoing strategy. The company prioritizes the well-being and development of its team above all else, the belief being that if employees are well taken care of, they will in turn provide exceptional service to customers, thereby creating a positive feedback loop that benefits the entire organization—employees become extensions of the brand.

And it works. The company invests heavily in employee development, offering continuous learning opportunities beyond an initial 200-plus hours of training in the first year (wow!), which empowers

# THERE'S NO REPLACEMENT FOR A BUSINESS FOLLOWING THROUGH ON ITS PROMISES TO APPLICANTS.

———

team members with the skills and knowledge they need to succeed ... even after they stop working for The Container Store. This commitment to employee growth fosters a sense of loyalty and pride among staff, as they feel valued and supported by their employer.

As you can imagine, this "employee-first" philosophy also significantly impacts employee retention. By creating a work environment where employees feel appreciated, engaged and motivated, the company significantly reduces their annual turnover. Over a recent five-year span (2019 to 2023), the organization maintained a lower turnover rate compared to industry norms and positioned itself as a leader in employee retention within the retail industry. This commitment and stability in their internal workforce is considered the main contributor to a consistent and high-quality customer experience, further reinforcing The Container Store's reputation as a great place to both work and shop.

That's the power of employee engagement. The Container Store proves that surrounding yourself with the right people—and taking care of them—is what keeps a brand at the top of its game.

### First Watch

Another fave brand of mine that predicates itself on focusing on their employees is First Watch: The Daytime Cafe. During my consulting days, I was lucky enough to spend time with the executive team of this popular breakfast, brunch and lunch concept on a variety of initiatives. But none of them was more fulfilling than being in the room when their two-word mission statement was born: "You First."

How powerful is that? Just two simple words, but with monumental impact to the recipients. Obviously, "You First" has the parallel ability to be focused on the dining guests *and* the employees. But really... I felt the intent was for the team members.

First Watch has several programs, technology and collateral that validate how serious they are about focusing on the employees, but one that really stands out to me is their takeaway pamphlet—available at the host stand for anyone to grab—with the bold tagline, "Join for the Hours, Stay for the People." A QR code on the pamphlet (when scanned) leads to the company's Careers webpage and lists a dozen attractive employee benefits, but not even the sell-line—"No Nights Ever"—comes close to capturing the company's real appeal or how potential team members must feel when they join the band. This simple piece of collateral may initially seem like a recruiting tool, but it becomes a bona fide retention strategy once employees get exposed to the daily "You First" engagement from company leaders.

There's no replacement for a business following through on its promises to the applicant during courtship.

### BambooHR

BambooHR, a human resource software company, stands out with its unique Paid Paid Vacation initiative. (That double "paid" was not a typo.) This program goes beyond standard paid time off by offering employees $2,000 annually to spend on vacation, provided they disconnect *entirely* from work during their time away. Call the office, send a work email, fire off a business text… lose the $2,000. Wow!

This initiative promotes work-life balance and shows the company's commitment to employee well-being and mental health, fostering a culture of trust and rejuvenation. This benefit shouts out "Employees First."

### Southwest Airlines

Another company widely known for its employee-first approach is Southwest Airlines. You would think that the focus is predominantly on the passengers, but as with The Container Store, the company believes that happy, engaged employees will, in turn, provide excellent customer service, which has always been key to Southwest's success.

One example is Southwest's profit-sharing program, which gives employees a share of the company's profits. This program is based on the principle that employees should directly benefit from the company's success, reinforcing their connection to the business's growth. This is huge for employees of the highly profitable airline. The profit-sharing program demonstrates Southwest's commitment to putting team members first by aligning their success with the company's financial performance.

When employees know that their efforts contribute directly to the company's success and that they will share in it, it boosts morale and engagement.

THESE INNOVATIVE BUSINESSES decided that the long-term health of their brand would be achieved through engaged team members. Some of the

# SHIFT YOUR BRAND TO EMPLOYEE-FIRST AND RESULTS WILL BE HERCULEAN.

———

employee-first initiatives I shared here are big expenses, and some are little-to-no-cost to the brand. But all of these companies see the undeniable value in making the employees the center of attention. And that's worth everything. Are there synapses firing off in your brain right now with questions like...

- How could you start shifting the spotlight to shine on your employees?

- What small, incremental shifts—or big initiatives—would be possible for the company leaders to immediately implement?

Shift your brand to an employee-first business, and the results will be Herculean.

# GREATEST HITS

**1 Put employees before end users—**
This mindset flips the traditional customer-first script and spotlights the real rock stars of the business: your team members.

**2 Empower leaders at every level—**
An employee-first culture starts when every leader, not just the executive team, feels responsible for the people experience.

**3 Deliver what you promise—**
When your promised value proposition for employees aligns with reality, you create lifelong fans.

You can't just hope
people will be okay—
you've got to give
them the tools and
support to be okay.

**DOLLY PARTON**

# CONSIDER UNIQUE BENEFITS AS A DIFFERENTIATOR

ONE OF my initial goals in writing *Engagement That Rocks* was to avoid talking at length about employee pay and benefits—as important as they are—since those elements are not really considered "engagement." Pay and benefits are both passive initiatives and are usually automatically implemented; employee engagement requires in-the-moment intentionality and active involvement from leaders. However, in the competitive landscape of today's business world, you *must* offer competitive salaries and a robust benefits package to attract and retain top talent. It's a part of enhancing the employee's experience. So, let's address it.

## PERKS THAT RESONATE

We are in an era of unique employee benefits. Company leaders have realized a critical part of initially setting themselves apart: offering the workforce perks that resonate on a deeper, more personal level. These benefits aren't just add-ons, either; they're fundamental to building a culture that rocks.

Consider the impact of providing benefits tailored to the needs and desires of your employees. It's not just about flashy perks like flexible work hours, mental health days, nap pods, ping-pong tables and free meals—although those can certainly turn heads—but about understanding and addressing the challenges and aspirations of your team.

Companies that excel in this specific area recognize that their people are their greatest asset, and by offering unique benefits, they differentiate themselves in a crowded market. As Willie Nelson once said, "Success is not about money. Success is about living a good life and taking care of your people." The best benefits send the message: *We genuinely care for the people behind the work.*

This chapter dives into the innovative strategies that forward-thinking organizations are implementing to create a workplace environment that appeals to potential hires and fosters motivation, loyalty and satisfaction among existing employees.

Just like a good opener at a concert, employee benefits prep the crowd for the main artists. Stellar pay and benefits are just the price of admission; authentic *engagement* is the headliner.

### Empyrean

At the invitation of my former colleague and now human resources executive James Stanton, I was fortunate to be the keynote speaker at Empyrean's annual conference a few years ago. With a purpose to "Build a Better Culture Through Benefits," this HR technology and benefits administration outsourcing company combines the most modern benefits tech with world-class, high-touch service and support. They are the "go-to" authority when it comes to what employees want.

As part of my due diligence with them, they shared with me their latest findings on the "Top Unique Company Benefits Desired by Today's Workforce." It was no surprise to see that "flexible work hours" and "remote work options" topped this post-pandemic list, but to see the meteoric importance of a few other benefits was eye opening—wellness programs, ongoing training and development opportunities, paid parental leave programs, free gym memberships, charitable volunteer programs, on-site childcare and even pet insurance and pet-friendly policies.

These preferred benefits validate how different today's workforce is from generations past. But even more so, how widely expected it is that companies offer these benefits. In addition to great pay and health insurance, perspective employees just assume benefits like these to be the norm for potential employers and are truly shocked when they discover they are not.

## INITIATIVES THAT MAKE YOU GO "HMMM"

As you consider ways to differentiate your business from competitors, let me rapid-fire share some interesting benefits programs and initiatives from industry leaders that may serve as a catalyst of possibility at your company.

### The Home Depot

Homeowner do-it-yourself king The Home Depot offers its employees a benefit called the Homer Fund, which is an internal charity that provides financial assistance to employees facing unexpected hardships. Since its inception, the program has distributed over $276 million to more than 185,000 associates and their families, delivering aid for crises such as illness, natural disasters, evictions and funeral costs.

# STELLAR PAY AND BENEFITS ARE THE PRICE OF ADMISSION; AUTHENTIC ENGAGEMENT IS THE HEADLINER.

——

### Nordstrom

Nordstrom, the big box department store that focuses on fashion and customer service, offers its employees a benefit called Personal Stylist. This program provides employees access to professional personal stylists who help employees curate work-appropriate wardrobes that align with their personal taste and the company's brand image. Part two of the program then offers free training and resources for team members to become certified personal stylists themselves.

### Clockwise

Time management software company Clockwise offers Focus Fridays, a unique program where the entire company clears its calendar of meetings every Friday. This dedicated, uninterrupted time allows everyone to focus deeply on their projects, tackle creative tasks or even step away from work for personal growth.

### Netflix

Streaming service icon Netflix offers its employees a benefit called Unlimited Parental Leave, which allows new parents to take as much time off as they need during the first year after a child's birth or adoption.

## Patagonia

Clothing and lifestyle brand Patagonia offers its employees what it calls Environmental Internships, which allow team members to take up to two months off from their normal job to work on an environmental project of their choosing, anywhere in the world. Patagonia may have a cult-like following of customers, but its employees are equally immersed.

## Guild Education

Guild Education, a company that partners with employers to offer education and upskilling opportunities for their employees, provides their *own* team members with a benefit called Education Stipend. Each employee may receive up to $5,000 per year to pursue their own educational goals and interests. This is a great example of a brand "walking the talk" of their mission—internally and externally—which keeps their employees engaged.

## Kaiser Permanente

Kaiser Permanente, a California-based health care company, offers its employees a program called Thrive, a comprehensive wellness program designed to promote healthy lifestyles and reduce stress. It offers a range of benefits and resources, such as fitness classes, healthy cooking demonstrations, stress-management workshops and smoking cessation programs. Thrive also includes an online platform with personalized wellness plans, tracking tools and access to a wellness coach for one-on-one support and guidance.

The program demonstrates a commitment to employee health and well-being while it recognizes that healthy employees are more productive, engaged and satisfied in their work. Obviously, this contributes to a culture of wellness and support within the organization, but it also helps to attract and retain top talent in the competitive health care industry.

### Salesforce

Technology and customer relations management software giant Salesforce offers its employees a Work from Anywhere policy, which allows team members to work remotely from anywhere in the world. This demonstrates the company's commitment to flexibility and work-life balance. If that weren't enough, Salesforce also has a benefit called Volunteer Time Off, through which employees can take paid time off to volunteer for causes they are passionate about. *Paid* time off.

## Navy Federal Credit Union

The not-for-profit financial institution Navy Federal
Credit Union, which serves members of the military
and their families, offers its team members a benefit
called the Live Your Life program, which is designed
to promote work-life balance and well-being. In
addition to amazing employee benefits, such as
flexible scheduling, telework options, on-site fitness
centers and wellness programs, the program includes
a concierge service that helps team members with
tasks such as dry cleaning, grocery shopping and meal
delivery, all designed to save time and reduce stress.
Live Your Life recognizes the challenges that military
families face, such as frequent moves and deployments,
and seeks to provide support and resources to help
employees manage their personal and professional
lives.

## 3M

Manufacturing behemoth 3M offers its employees a
benefit called 15 Percent Culture, which encourages
team members to spend 15 percent of their time on
projects that are outside of their regular job and job
responsibilities but aligned with the company's values
and goals. That's an interesting and gutsy approach,

since many other employers would certainly fear they would be supporting and paying for their staff to take company time to find their passions elsewhere and potentially leave. But risk-adverse 3M gets it. And their employees are engaged.

### Lush Cosmetics

Lush Cosmetics, the popular personal-care company that specializes in handmade, ethical and sustainable beauty products, offers its employees a benefit called Charity Pot, which donates 100 percent of the proceeds from the sale of a specific product to local grassroots organizations working on environmental, animal welfare and human rights issues.

### Nugget Markets

Nugget Markets, a family-owned grocery chain, gives every employee access to free life coaching services. Certainly not every Nugget Market team member will take advantage of this perk, but what about the ones who don't? Even they feel the value in what the company does for its employees.

### Raising Cane's Chicken Fingers

Raising Cane's Chicken Fingers, known for its delectable chicken fingers and cult-like following, has also garnered attention for its pioneering efforts to support its managers. Recognizing the importance of stability and satisfaction of an employee-first philosophy, the company has implemented a remarkable initiative to help managers become homeowners.

One standout feature of this program is the brand's generous offering of a $10,000 closing-costs payment for restaurant leaders purchasing their first home. This significant financial aid helps alleviate the substantial upfront costs associated with buying a home, making the dream of homeownership more attainable for many managers. It certainly isn't the only retention benefit the brand offers, but by investing in their managers' futures, Raising Cane's fosters a deep sense of loyalty and commitment, which translates into a more dedicated workforce. The benefit not only enhances employee satisfaction but also contributes to the company's reputation for excellent service and a strong, supportive culture.

THE REALITY of today is that companies *must* have great benefits in place for any hope of attracting top-tier talent. So, your brand may already be a step behind. Depending on your role in the organization, you may have no control over your company's offered benefits anyway, but I wanted you to at least be aware of the baseline of today's expectations.

Still, there is hope beyond great pay and benefits. Remember, price of admission is no longer good enough. Employees need more.

# GREATEST HITS

1 **Go beyond pay and perks**—Long-term loyalty comes from meaningful amplifiers, not just "price of admission" basics. Employees crave more.

2 **Tailor benefits to what really matters to your people**—Innovative benefits reflect employee values and show you're listening, which leads to loyalty.

3 **Benefits alone don't drive engagement**—Standout company perks definitely turn heads, but authentic culture is what keeps people around.

You do not merely want
to be considered just
the best of the best. You
want to be considered
the only ones who do
what you do.

**JERRY GARCIA
(THE GRATEFUL DEAD)**

# MAKE IT
## ABOUT THEM

T**HE NATURE** of work has changed. And the expectations of today's workforce have shifted right along with it. If you're still stuck in the old-school, micromanagement, clock-in-at-nine, grind-all-day mindset, then it's time to adjust your perspective. Because here's the thing—and this may seem controversial—it's *their world now.* The employees are in control, and the spotlight is on *them.* The power dynamics have shifted, and if you're not adapting to this new mindset, you're going to miss the opportunities to attract or keep top talent.

For better or worse, welcome to the new era of work—the *employee revolution.*

## EMPLOYEES ARE THE SHOW

Unfortunately, the pandemic changed the game for good. The old ways of working—long commutes, set work hours, rigid schedules—have been replaced with something more flexible, more creative and sometimes even more painful for employers. Employees are the "show" now... and they're looking for an employer who understands them and knows how to engage with them.

In the United States, talent is scarce, and at the time of this writing, unemployment is low. But these points apply even in situations where unemployment is high. The era of "do it our way or hit the road" is over. Team members want their work lives to revolve around them and their personal style.

Employees also have more options than ever. If you're not giving them what they need, they'll go find it somewhere else—be it with a competitor, on a freelance gig or in a totally different industry. And that "somewhere else" might be remote or part-time, because employees are playing their own game now. They are looking for more than just a paycheck—they're looking for freedom; the freedom to live their own work-life-balance equation. You might not be able to provide them with the exact freedom they desire, but the competition for talent is fierce. If you don't adapt, your workforce is going to be anemic. It makes you wonder...

- How does a brand handle this radical shift?
- How do you adjust to the way employees want to work?

Let's start with understanding and addressing the top three critical employee-centric needs that would position your business as an employer-of-choice:

1 Remote work and flexibility
2 Accepted individuality
3 Authentic listening

## REMOTE WORK AND FLEXIBILITY ARE CRITICAL

I wanted so badly to stay away from addressing "remote work hours" and "flex schedules" in this book for one main reason: I know most jobs won't be able to provide these specific options to employees. However, I must mention them, since both benefits are at the top of the list for today's workforce and are perceived to be the best ways to keep people engaged.

Remote work and flexibility aren't just nice bonuses anymore—they're the Holy Grail of benefits. Employees are more interested in getting the job done on their own terms than they are in adhering to a rigid schedule. Are you more of a night owl than a morning bird? Then work from midnight to 8 a.m., if that's when your creativity peaks. Would you be more productive working from home than in an office? Then stay home with the dog and work in your pajamas, if that will help your productivity. The idea: Trust that the work will get done.

Even if these are unrealistic options for your specific type of business, perhaps implementing a hybrid model or "flex hours" approach to scheduling and working would be enough of an attractive benefit for many potential hires.

### Ford Motor Company

Ford Motor Company embraced this forward-thinking approach to workplace flexibility by transitioning from its traditional brick-and-mortar model to a hybrid work strategy. The company allows all 25,000 salaried employees who don't require on-site presence to split their time between home and office settings. The strategy includes the development of "collaboration centers" at locations like its Dearborn headquarters and other major facilities, where the spaces are equipped with dual-monitor setups, adjustable desks, video conferencing tools and even meditation areas.

These changes have enhanced productivity and work-life balance for the team members, who have

# EMPLOYEES THAT CAN BRING THEIR FULL SELVES TO WORK PERFORM AT A HIGHER LEVEL.

———

cited reduced commute times and fewer workplace distractions.

## Target

American retail giant Target has also moved to a hybrid work model, particularly for its corporate workforce. Until a few years ago, the company operated from a traditional office-centric approach, especially in its downtown Minneapolis headquarters. However, in response to evolving work trends, Target transitioned to a hybrid model, reducing its physical office footprint while creating "flex floors" at HQ. These spaces allow employees to use temporary desks and flexible meeting areas, promoting collaboration during in-office days, while supporting remote work. The policy also allows individuals to decide when to work remotely or come to the office.

To maintain a sense of community and connection, Target introduced periodic "core weeks," during which employees are encouraged to gather at the office for major company events or milestones, such as quarterly earnings announcements or the national fall meeting. It's the best of both worlds, as the employees have their preferred work-life balance, and the company still manages to produce results and perpetuate the culture.

THESE EMPLOYEE-CENTRIC ideas around remote work and flex hours are about team members expecting employers to trust them to produce results, where and when they want. Certainly, they're not ideal for *every* company, but this is where we are. At the very least, these initiatives should get the brain synapses firing on what *might* be possible, knowing their importance to today's workforce. The brutal truth is this: Do nothing and you run the risk of shrinking your available talent pool.

## ROCK YOUR OWN STYLE

Just like in a band where each member brings their own sound, employees today want to express their individuality. Having a personal identity that doesn't conform to any particular set of rules or guidelines is a high-value need of today's entry-level workers. And it's not just about what they do—it's about who they are. From their hairstyles, to their tattoos and piercings, to how they dress and communicate with the boss, employees are demanding that the workplace respects their personal style. As Janis Joplin once put it, "Don't compromise yourself. You are all you've got." That raw truth resonates deeply with today's workforce—they want to bring their authentic selves to work without fear of being molded into something they're not.

If your dress code still leans toward stuffy suits and ties, it might be time to swap that out for a more relaxed, authentic look. A casual dress code is no longer just about comfort—it's about embracing who people are. If visible tattoos are still a non-starter for your company, you may want to revisit that approach, since more people are getting inked up today than ever before... and these "walking pieces of art" may be the exact rock stars you need in your business. If a formal hierarchy stands in the way of having an open conversation with the top leadership, then maybe it's time to take a sledgehammer to that process and open up a direct line of communication. Employees expect transparency and an ear.

### Condado Tacos

Ohio-based restaurant concept Condado Tacos has a relaxed approach to uniforms, which reflects its emphasis on individuality and employee comfort. Rather than requiring employees to wear traditional uniforms, the company encourages team members to dress in a way that feels authentic to them, allowing for personal expression. In this "come as you are" culture, employees can wear casual attire such as jeans,

T-shirts, athleisure wear or other comfortable clothing that aligns with their personal style. As long as their nametag is visible, they can wear what they want.

I GET IT... some of you are completely freaking out right now at the thought of relaxing some of these policies for the sake of a workforce's desires, but a team member's individuality has become a critical part of staying loyal to a brand.

**So, what could you do? What would attract and retain top talent, yet still hold true to your company's values?**

I spent a lot of time detailing this business issue in my first book, *Culture That Rocks*, because there were not a lot of companies that were fostering these types of liberties among their employee base at that time, but I have since seen a big shift in what brands allow. And with great results. When employees can bring their full selves to work, they'll perform at a higher level.

Renaissance painter and sculptor Michelangelo made a similar comparison more than 500 years ago, when he described his process for sculpting a piece of art. He famously stated that he never actually created a single statue; all he did was chip away at the excess rock to reveal what was *already* inside. Allowing team members to have this much freedom of self-expression does the same thing—it creates unique living pieces of art. And unique people create unique experiences for customers.

## LISTEN AND ADAPT

Top-down, one-way communication is one of the fastest routes to disengagement. Employees need a voice; better yet, they need leaders to listen. To avoid employees mentally checking out, business leaders must develop the high-priority art of authentic listening. To assist them in this skill-building effort, forward-thinking companies have implemented various "employee listening" programs to help team members feel valued. These feedback forums could be an open dialogue, but the goal is to truly listen to the employees and effectively address workplace issues.

### Synchrony

Consumer financial services company Synchrony is an innovative brand when it comes to employee listening. Senior leaders regularly host open forums,

# TOP-DOWN, ONE-WAY COMMUNICATION IS ONE OF THE FASTEST ROUTES TO DISENGAGEMENT.

——————

including "Ask Us Anything" meetings that encourage system-wide transparency and give employees a platform to voice their concerns or questions directly to executives. This single initiative has been so widely applauded by Synchrony's workforce that the company goes a step further by conducting smaller, targeted meetings to explore specific issues and co-create solutions with team members.

WHETHER YOUR company has formal or informal listening initiatives, the obvious goals are to seek out and pay attention to your team's feedback, tune in to what they need and then evolve your policies accordingly. Authentic listening can create a more engaged and satisfied workforce, with their direct input shaping organizational changes and policies. Tapping into my inner Janet Jackson, that type of environment is "like a moth to a flame" for current and potential employees.

My advice: Listen and reap (the rewards).

## QUIET QUITTING

Lack of listening to employees leads to one of the most significant challenges companies face today: *quiet quitting*—a phenomenon that's on the rise as team members mentally disengage from their jobs.

Quiet quitting is like when a member of the band plays just enough to stay in the group but isn't really invested in the music. They're there, but they're checked out. In a way, it's a silent protest; a direct result of employers who fail to listen or adjust to the evolving needs of their workforce. Over time, employees working in this type of environment will emotionally disconnect from the company's mission and feel undervalued in their role.

As a leader, if you see quiet quitting creeping into your band of employees, it's time for some active engagement... which includes authentic listening. Seek feedback and set up some "open mic" listening sessions. Regular check-ins, employee surveys and a commitment to act on the feedback are great ways to eliminate the problem of team members existing in a zombie-like state.

In today's world, employees want to feel that they matter beyond their productivity. They want their voices heard and they want to be seen. When you respect your employees and engage with them, quiet quitting becomes a thing of the past.

## "I'M THE BOSS OF ME"

The era of employee-driven power is here, and the spotlight is on your people. They're the stars of the show, and if you want your company to rock, you need to adjust to their tune. Or as Dave Grohl reminds us, "No one is you, and that is your power." That uniqueness is what fuels creativity, builds culture and sets your brand apart from the rest. To stay in sync with today's workforce, you've got to *make it about them*.

**Are you ready to lead in this new world of work—the employee revolution?**

Flexibility, individuality and communication are the names of the game. If you give your employees the freedom to be their own authentic selves, they'll bring the energy and creativity that will make your company iconic.

## GREATEST HITS

**1** **Champion flexibility**—If you want top talent to stick around, you've got to offer freedom over where, when and how they work.

**2** **Celebrate individuality**—Your people aren't robots, so embrace their diverse personalities; when you let them bring their full selves to work, everyone wins.

**3** **Listen and adapt**—Employees want to be seen and heard, and companies that tune in will outlast the ones that tune out.

True stars shine
brightest when they feel
seen, heard and valued
by the people around
them.

**STEVIE NICKS
(FLEETWOOD MAC)**

# OFFER LEADERSHIP WITH A HEART

IN THE world of leadership, there's an old adage that still rings true: People don't leave jobs; they leave people. In fact, a 1998 Gallup survey verified this. The global survey of two million employees, across multiple industries, over 25 years revealed that the number one reason employees leave (or stay) at a company is because of leadership—specifically, their direct supervisor. Fast-forward to Gallup's 2024 *Indicator* report, and they found that 37 percent of employees cited "lack of engagement" and "culture issues" as their main reasons for bailing—both of which are direct leadership outcomes. These results are reminders that the way you treat team members affects their engagement, loyalty and performance.

If you want to create a workplace culture that truly rocks, it begins with leading from the heart. Leaders who trade command-and-control tactics for support-and-coach approaches build trust, respect and genuine relationships with their teams. This is especially true during those crucial one-on-one interactions.

## THE HEART-CENTERED APPROACH

Leadership isn't about barking orders; it's about being present and supportive. Your job as a leader isn't to have all the answers but to ask the right questions, remove obstacles and empower your team to thrive. All of these techniques enhance employee engagement.

### Tommy Spaulding

In Tommy Spaulding's perfectly named book *The Heart-Led Leader*, Tommy advocates for exactly this: a leadership style centered on authenticity and emotional connection. He emphasizes that true leaders operate from the heart, valuing qualities such as humility, vulnerability, empathy and love. His book explores the "18-inch journey"—the distance between the head and the heart—encouraging leaders to move beyond intellect and foster deeper emotional connections in their personal and professional lives.

I'm a huge fan of Tommy's and multiple times have seen him speak onstage, where he uses compelling stories from his own experiences and interactions with exceptional leaders to illustrate the transformative power of heart-led leadership. This philosophy not only enhances workplace culture but also meaningfully impacts the lives of others, driving lasting success and fulfillment for both leaders and their teams.

A boss who truly cares about me as a person? Yes, please.

### Susan Steinbrecher

Before Tommy Spaulding's masterpiece, there was my friend Susan Steinbrecher with her opus, *Heart-Centered Leadership: Lead Well, Live Well.* Co-written with Joel Bennett, this business and leadership guide emphasizes the importance of authenticity, self-care and mindfulness in fostering a thriving workplace. Her book also takes a kinder, gentler approach to leadership by presenting seven principles and virtues that encourage leaders to cultivate emotional connections, ethical practices and a people-centered approach to management. It's a fantastic blueprint for those looking to adjust their leadership style.

Drawing on interviews, case studies, scientific insights and practical exercises, *Heart-Centered Leadership* illustrates how leading with the heart can inspire employees, improve workplace satisfaction and enhance profitability by retaining top talent. This leadership philosophy integrates personal growth and professional success to address challenges in modern business... and engaged employees are the ultimate by-product.

### Badger Balm

Badger Balm, a family-owned skincare brand in New Hampshire, is a perfect example of a heart-centered approach. They live by their mission of kindness and empathy. Their leaders prioritize connecting with employees on a personal level, holding regular "wellness chats" to check in about how team members are doing mentally, emotionally and physically—not to discuss deadlines or quotas. Well-being is the sole purpose of the discussion.

This mindset shift from authoritative boss to supportive coach improves morale and creates a sense of psychological safety. Employees perform better when they know their leaders care about them as people, not just as workers.

# EMPLOYEES PERFORM BETTER WHEN THEY KNOW THEIR LEADERS CARE ABOUT THEM AS PEOPLE.

———

### Denny's

In April 2023, Denny's, the global restaurant chain of 1,600-plus locations, launched a free Mental Health and Wellness Summit series designed to promote mental health awareness and provide resources to the public. The summits offered both virtual and in-person participation, making them accessible to a wide audience. The initiative was part of the company's broader commitment to holistic wellness, addressing both personal and workplace mental health challenges, which the COVID-19 pandemic had heightened. The first summit featured many accredited doctors, keynote speakers and a leading expert on mental health, mindful eating and workplace wellness.

Denny's CEO, Kelli Valade, highlighted the importance of these efforts, stating, "Denny's has always been committed to feeding people's bodies, minds and souls. Now is the time to think about how we can bring our whole selves to all facets of our lives, including the workplace."

Separately, results from a 2023 American Psychological Association survey showed that 59 percent of employees (or three in five) experienced negative impacts of work-related stress. Additionally, 87 percent of employees thought that actions from employers would help their mental health. Denny's leadership recognized this need from their workforce and decided to act—hence, the summits. Even better, Denny's took it to the streets and opened up their initiative to the general public. This is the type of heart-centered approach we need in business.

## TRUST: THE CURRENCY OF LEADERSHIP

Trust is the currency of great leadership. You earn it through transparency, consistency and genuinely valuing your team's input. I have seen many programs and assessments identify "trust" as the single most important characteristic that people want in a leader. Once an employee loses trust in a boss, the relationship is irreparable.

There are a few practical things you can do to build trust with the team.

**Be transparent and honest**—Trust thrives on transparency. Leaders should openly communicate about company goals, challenges and decisions. When employees feel informed, they're less likely to speculate or feel disconnected.

- Share company updates regularly through town halls, emails or informal chats.

- Be honest about challenges, even if the news isn't ideal. People appreciate honesty over sugar-coated messages.

- Admit mistakes. Showing vulnerability humanizes leaders and builds credibility.

**Follow through on commitments**—A leader's words should match their actions. When you say you'll do something, follow through. Broken promises can quickly erode trust.

- Avoid overpromising—only commit to what you can realistically deliver.

- Update employees on progress related to any commitments, even if delays occur.

- Demonstrate accountability by meeting deadlines and owning up to oversights.

**Show empathy and care**—Employees trust leaders who genuinely care about them as individuals, not just as workers. Empathy strengthens relationships and fosters a supportive environment.

- Take time to check in with employees, both professionally and personally.

- Be understanding about personal challenges and provide flexibility where possible.

- Recognize and celebrate individual and team milestones.

**Empower employees and involve them in decisions—** Trust grows when employees feel their voices are valued and their input matters. Empowering them to take ownership fosters confidence in leadership.

- Actively seek employee input on decisions that affect their work.

- Delegate responsibilities, allowing team members to lead initiatives.

- Celebrate their successes and recognize their contributions.

## THE SIX-MONTH RULE

Although my career with Hard Rock started as a restaurant host, once I was promoted to manager, I had to adjust my relationship with the rest of the team. As many of you know, internal promotions are a fine line to walk. One day, you're seating guests at a colleague's table; the next day, you become their supervisor and have to hold them accountable for their actions.

Before my ascent into leadership, I made a cognizant choice to keep the staff's trust factor high with me by making a singular, secret decision: Unless it was a terminable offense, I would *not* write up any Hard Rocker for infractions during my first six months of management. Late to work, eating in the side station, chewing gum in front of guests, incorrect uniform standards... I let *all* of it slide. Granted, I still had the side-bar conversation with the employee, but I did not formalize it by writing it down in their employee file. Instead, my language was more of a casual, "C'mon man... you know we get in trouble for that. Let's be cool about it so I don't eventually have to write you up. That would suck."

Over time, I built that trust up enough so that when my six-month mark hit as a manager, it was so much easier to then start holding people accountable for their actions. The trust factor was high between me and the staff; so much so that most of them felt they were letting *me* down by breaking the rules.

I'm not sure if this approach would work for you (or if it's even correct), but it shows another real-world perspective on how to build trust with team members.

## RESPECT: THE OTHER SIDE OF THE COIN

Along with trust, "respect" is the twin pillar of leadership—when employees feel respected, they show up for you in ways that go beyond their job description. And there are many ways a leader can amp up respect with employees.

**Lead by example**—Employees respect leaders who walk the talk and model the behavior they expect from others. Demonstrating integrity, professionalism and a strong work ethic inspires others to follow suit. Some examples:

- Show up on time, prepared and ready to contribute, just as you expect from your team.

- Demonstrate a commitment to company values and uphold them, even in tough situations.

- Treat everyone—from executives to entry-level employees—with the same level of respect and fairness.

**Recognize and value contributions**—Employees feel respected when their efforts are acknowledged and their skills are valued. Regular recognition reinforces that their work matters and motivates them to keep performing at their best.

- Provide specific, genuine feedback when recognizing employees' achievements.

- Celebrate team and individual successes publicly, in meetings or via email.

- Offer growth opportunities, such as training or new responsibilities, to show you value their potential.

**Treat employees as partners, not subordinates**—Respect is built when employees feel like they are part of the process, not just following orders. When leaders collaborate and value input, it creates mutual respect.

- Actively seek employee opinions during decision-making processes, especially for policies that affect them.

- Encourage open dialogue and listen without judgment.

- Share credit for successes with the team and be transparent about challenges.

## MOD Pizza

One standout example is MOD Pizza, a fast-casual pizza company that embraces "servant leadership" as part of its culture. Managers at MOD are trained to serve their employees—many who are physically disabled or formerly incarcerated—first, ensuring their needs are met so that they can serve customers effectively.

This approach has led to a highly engaged and loyal workforce where members of the MOD Squad (their employees) feel seen, heard and supported. And in turn, that loyalty has parlayed into unforgettable customer experiences, helping propel MOD to one of the great company cultures in the United States today.

## Dan Campbell

Detroit Lions head coach Dan Campbell has completely transformed the culture of the NFL team into one of accountability, camaraderie and resilience. But at the heart of his leadership style is respect.

Since his arrival as head coach in 2021, Campbell has prioritized creating a "self-regulating" team environment, where players set and uphold their own standards of performance and behavior. By empowering team leaders and fostering trust and respect, Campbell has shifted focus from a

# EMPLOYEES THAT FEEL RESPECTED, SUPPORTED AND VALUED WILL WALK THROUGH WALLS FOR YOU.

———

coach-centric approach to one where players take ownership of their success. And it shows. On the sidelines. In the locker room. During media events.

This cultural overhaul has resulted in a closer-knit team—which most players now call "family"—and improved performance on the field, including a remarkable turnaround in recent seasons. This renaissance is 100 percent due to Campbell's leadership style. Marked by passion, authenticity and emotional connection, this environment of trust and respect has deeply resonated with both players and fans, driving the Lions' resurgence as a competitive force in the league.

## THE POWER OF ONE-ON-ONES

Department meetings or all-staff gatherings are great for a lot of reasons, but the magic of leadership often happens in one-on-one moments with an employee. Whether it's a performance review, a coaching session or an informal chat, these interactions are opportunities to build connection and trust.

Here are some best practices for heart-centered one-on-ones:

- **Be fully present**—Put down your phone, close your laptop and give your full attention. These moments matter.

- **Ask open-ended questions**—Instead of saying, "How's it going?" try, "What's the most rewarding and challenging part of your work right now?"

- **Listen actively**—Reflect back what you hear and acknowledge emotions. As we discussed earlier, authentic listening is one of the most powerful acts of leadership.

- **End with encouragement**—Even during tough conversations, find a way to uplift and inspire your employee to move forward confidently.

### Sweetgreen

Sweetgreen, the fast-casual salad chain, offers a great example of effective one-on-ones. Leaders there use regular, individual meetings not just to review performance but also to discuss employees' long-term goals. And the conversations go much deeper than the usual, "Where do you see yourself in five years?" By focusing on real personal and professional growth, Sweetgreen fosters loyalty and motivation.

The extra time it will take to have these one-on-one discussions will be worth the commitment in the long term. Try it and watch the team's engagement flourish.

## PRACTICAL STEPS TO LEAD WITH HEART

Let's boil this down into some actionable steps. Here are just a few suggestions:

- **Create a culture of feedback**—Encourage open dialogue where employees feel safe sharing ideas and concerns.

- **Celebrate small wins**—Recognition doesn't always have to be a grand gesture; a simple "thank you" or shout-out can go a long way.

- **Show empathy during challenges**—When employees struggle, your response can define their experience; lead with understanding and support.

- **Invest in development**—Offer training, mentorship and growth opportunities that demonstrate you're invested in their future.

### King Arthur Baking Company

One fantastic company that exemplifies heart-centered leadership in all these areas is King Arthur Baking Company. As a 100 percent employee-owned business, the company ensures that every team member has a tangible stake in its success, fostering a sense of shared purpose and accountability. One of their standout practices is regularly briefing employees on the company's financial health and strategic goals. This transparency builds trust and empowers employees to contribute meaningfully. Additionally, King Arthur offers extensive professional development opportunities, demonstrating their investment in team members' growth.

By aligning business goals with employee well-being, King Arthur Baking creates a culture of respect, trust and engagement—proving that when you treat your people well, they'll help you rise to any occasion. (See what I did there?)

### Barry-Wehmiller

Another inspiring example is Barry-Wehmiller, a global manufacturing company based in St. Louis, Missouri. While their industry might not scream "people-first culture," BW's approach to leadership does. Their

"Truly Human Leadership" philosophy focuses on treating employees like family, especially with their standout program, Listening Circles. During these structured group discussions, employees openly share challenges and ideas in a judgment-free space. Leaders are trained to listen actively, without interrupting or steering the conversation, fostering an environment of trust and mutual respect.

In addition, Barry-Wehmiller prioritizes personal growth through its BW Leadership Institute, where employees are taught principles of empathetic leadership. This isn't limited to management; all team members are invited to participate, ensuring that leadership skills permeate every level of the company. The results? Employees report feeling valued not just for what they do but also for who they are, leading to a more unified culture, lower turnover and (you guessed it) higher engagement.

Barry-Wehmiller proves that a heart-led approach works—even in the world of manufacturing.

HEART-CENTERED LEADERSHIP isn't about being soft or avoiding tough decisions. It's about balancing strength with compassion, authority with empathy and vision with humanity. When employees feel respected, supported and valued, they'll walk through walls for you. As Chris Cornell so powerfully reminded us, "If you don't stand for something, you'll fall for anything." In business, that "something" takes the form of trust, respect and genuine care—without it, even your best talent will find another stage to play on. So, ask yourself…

- Is your company's leadership heart-centered?
- Are *you* leading with heart?

If not, now's the time to start. After all, great leadership isn't just about what you achieve; it's about how you make your people feel along the way. Build a culture that rocks—one heart-centered interaction at a time.

# GREATEST HITS

**1  Lead with humanity, not hierarchy—**
Ditch command-and-control tactics for trust, empathy and emotional connection to truly engage your team.

**2  Build trust like it's your main job—**
Consistency, transparency and genuine care are the currency of leadership that lasts.

**3  Turn up the volume on listening—**
One-way communication is out; truly listening, authentic feedback and employee-based action keep the band engaged.

The beautiful thing
about learning is that
nobody can take it
away from you.

**B.B. KING**

# PROVIDE A DEVELOPMENTAL SET LIST

I F YOUR workplace is a stage, then your employees are the rock stars. But even the greatest rock icons need rehearsals, inspiration and time to refine their craft. In business, this translates into intentional development—both personal and professional. To keep your team members engaged and motivated, you need to provide a developmental "set list" that offers diverse opportunities for growth.

It's not just about teaching job skills, either; it's about showing employees that you care about their future, both inside and outside of your organization. A world-class culture isn't built on stagnant teams. It's built on leaders who actively support learning and create paths for upward mobility.

## WHY DOES IT MATTER?

Picture this: You're a guitarist in a band that plays the same ten songs every night. Eventually, you'll lose interest, right? Employees feel the same way when they're stuck doing the same tasks, day in and day out, without any opportunities to grow. Development isn't just a perk; it's a necessity for keeping employees engaged, loyal and invested in your mission.

Many statistics prove that "employee development" directly impacts your company's ability to innovate and adapt. A 2022 *Harvard Business Review* article revealed that organizations with strong development programs see 34 percent higher retention rates compared to those without. That same year, Society of Human Resource Management's *Workplace Learning and Development* report highlighted that 76 percent of interviewed employees said they are more likely to stay with a company that offers continuous training and development opportunities. When team members expand their skills and knowledge, they bring fresh perspectives and creative solutions to the table.

Finally, investing in a person's growth sends a clear message: *We value you.* By prioritizing development, companies not only build a more capable workforce but also create a culture that inspires loyalty, innovation and long-term success.

You may already have some phenomenal programs in place at your company, but in my line of work, I get exposed to a lot of innovative and awe-inspiring programs that go beyond the normal management training program or individual development form. Besides, to create a comprehensive development program, you need to offer a variety of options; not every employee learns or grows in the same way, so a one-size-fits-all approach won't cut it. Here are some standout formats.

## INTERNAL DEVELOPMENT PROGRAMS

Internal development programs help employees fine-tune their skills and prepare for bigger gigs within the company. Whether through in-house training, workshops or certifications, internal growth opportunities amplify talent while reinforcing your company's mission and values.

### HubSpot

HubSpot, a leading inbound marketing software company and customer platform that connects a company's marketing, sales and service, offers one of the best internal growth development programs in business: HubSpot Academy. This comprehensive, in-house training platform offers free online courses, certifications and resources across various disciplines, including inbound marketing, sales, customer service and leadership development. Employees can access a wide range of interactive content, such as webinars, tutorials and hands-on exercises, enabling them to deepen their knowledge and expertise in their current roles or prepare for new challenges within the company.

### Patreon

Patreon, a membership platform that helps creators earn a sustainable income, also does this well, but in a more informal process. Their leadership simply focuses on learning through real-world experiences by encouraging employees to take on stretch assignments. For example, an employee from the product team could take on a project in the marketing department to develop a new user acquisition strategy. This would push the team member outside their usual scope of work and give them the chance to apply their skills in a new context while gaining experience in a different area. The company also hosts internal workshops and speaker events, allowing employees to learn from both internal leaders and external experts. Although these are not as formalized as HubSpot Academy, Patreon provides growth opportunities for team members to develop . . . and that's what employee engagement is about.

# TO CREATE AN ARMY OF PROMOTABLE GIANTS, DEVELOP EMPLOYEES BEYOND THEIR JOB DESCRIPTION.

---

### Hard Rock International

Now, for the other extreme. During my time leading Hard Rock's learning and development initiatives, my team created what I believe to be one of the greatest internal development programs on the planet. Okay, so I'm a little biased, but let me share with you some of the elements that allowed Hard Rockers to take ownership of their development.

For knowledge building, we created these programs:

- **ROCK U**—A self-directed, online corporate university, consisting of over 25 customized e-learning courses and over 50 online Harvard leadership courses.

- **Rockipedia**—The company's intranet-based tool of all things Hard Rock; every company policy, procedure, form and trivia that exists, in one completely searchable place. (Imagine keeping up with *that* data.)

For knowledge testing, we created these programs:

- **Hard Rock SATs (Self-Accountability Tests)**—A series of tests consisting of hundreds of questions regarding the company in every major discipline. Employees could take the SATs as often as they wanted if they did not like the score they received in any area; since the goal was knowledge retention, everyone won in that situation.

- **Hard Rock 360**—An internally created, online, 360-degree feedback assessment (consisting of leadership perceptions from the manager's boss, direct reports, peers and themselves). The questions and results were based exclusively on the company's internal and desired leadership behaviors. As a companion resource to the 360-degree assessment, each leadership behavior came with its own series of activities that could be completed to strengthen the manager's leadership quality being developed.

Any one of these development programs would have been a fantastic stand-alone resource, but in concert with each other, they became a part of Hard Rock's overall performance development process. Once these tools were widely accepted, they morphed into the annual performance review for leaders. Along with a manager's specific property financial results, their individual SAT scores and 360-degree feedback all pre-populated into an online performance review. The overall data became the perfect pre-cursor to the manager then completing and working on an Individual Development Plan. It was awesome! Over time, we discovered many leaders dipping into the various tools on their own throughout the year in their quest to constantly build up their knowledge base, improve their test scores and become promotable... which was the ultimate goal.

Carlos Santana nailed it when he said, "You can reinvent yourself every day. That's the secret." These initiatives gave our people the freedom and tools to do just that.

## MENTORSHIP PROGRAMS

Mentorship programs pair seasoned pros with rising stars for guidance and support. These relationships help employees navigate challenges, build confidence and chart a clear path forward in their careers. A formal mentor program ensures consistency and measurable outcomes. I dedicated an entire chapter to mentorship in my book, *Leadership That Rocks*, where I highlighted that 70 percent of all Fortune 500 companies had a formalized program in place. There is obvious, huge value in this developmental format.

### General Electric

General Electric has long been known for its mentorship initiatives, where leaders actively develop talent through one-on-one coaching. This program fosters personalized guidance, allowing employees to refine their skills, set meaningful career goals and build confidence. Studied by businesses everywhere, GE cultivates a pipeline of future leaders while strengthening relationships between employees and management.

## PAID LEARNING

Offering paid development like certifications, online courses and tuition reimbursement lets employees expand their repertoire and shows them you're truly invested in their growth. By taking care of the program costs, a company encourages employees to develop expertise that benefits them and the company. That's a win-win situation.

### Starbucks

Starbucks really took the lead on this approach with their College Achievement Plan, which provides full tuition coverage for employees pursuing a bachelor's degree online through Arizona State University. Fully paid! Surprisingly, employees who take advantage of the plan do not have to choose a degree even remotely related to Starbucks's industry. They can pursue their own academic interests, whether related to business, arts or other fields.

### Wegmans

Grocery store chain Wegmans offers a unique development program where deli- and butcher-department employees take trips overseas to visit farms, fisheries and artisan producers. These company-funded, immersive experiences allow team members to deepen their knowledge of sourcing, quality and cultural traditions, which they can then share with customers. By investing in these life-changing journeys, Wegmans reinforces its commitment to employee growth and delivering exceptional service.

## SELF-TAUGHT PROGRAMS

Providing access to self-directed learning resources, such as e-learning platforms or funding for educational materials, empowers employees to learn at their own pace. These programs promote autonomy and help team members build skills aligned with their personal and professional goals.

## Zappos

Online shoe retailer Zappos uses its Skills Accelerator program to empower employees to take charge of their career growth through self-directed learning. The program offers access to courses and the opportunity to shadow other departments, equipping team members with new skills and insights. By focusing on both vertical and lateral development, Zappos prepares employees for promotions or seamless transitions to other roles within the organization.

## Shopify

E-commerce-platform giant Shopify takes it a step further and provides each of its employees with an annual learning and development budget of $5,000 to invest in self-directed educational resources, including courses, conferences, coaching and even books. The program encourages continuous growth and skill-building, tailored to each individual's career goals and interests, and ensures that employees have ample opportunities to enhance their skills and grow professionally.

## DEPARTMENT CROSS-TRAINING

Walking in other team members' shoes is the ultimate remix—giving employees the chance to explore different departments, broaden their skill sets and better understand the entire business. Cross-training prepares employees to step into new roles when needed, increasing agility within the organization. It also enhances collaboration.

### Ritz-Carlton

As part of its famous Gold Standards training program, Ritz-Carlton fosters a cross-training program to ensure their associates are equipped to deliver exceptional service across multiple departments. Having a front desk agent train as a bellman or a concierge associate spend time as a housekeeper amplifies a variety of outcomes. Because peers have walked in each other's shoes, the initiative enhances operational flexibility, empowers team members to step into various roles as needed and maintains the brand's legendary service standards. Highly encouraged by leadership, cross-training is one of the best programs Ritz-Carlton employs to ensure "ladies and gentlemen serve ladies and gentlemen."

### Nick's Pizza and Pub

Nick Sarillo, founder of Chicago-based Nick's Pizza and Pub, operates his multi-floored, high-volume pizza restaurant like a leadership factory. The brand's unique culture emphasizes trust and empowerment, which includes *self-directed* cross-training for any interested team member. Nick implemented self-managed job duties, posted pay structures for every position and instituted a leadership certification process that allows employees to grow (both personally and professionally) at their own pace. Want to make more money? Want to move into a leadership role? Go for it! The various programs are spelled out and waiting for you at any time.

## APPRENTICESHIPS AND ROTATIONAL PROGRAMS

A bit more formalized, apprenticeships and rotational programs provide employees with hands-on experience in different roles, discovering new talents while building a versatile playlist of skills. These programs are especially valuable for preparing future leaders for any challenge.

### Unilever

More formalized than Nick's Pizza and Pub's process and more time-intensive than Ritz-Carlton's program, the Future Leaders Program was created by global consumer goods company Unilever. This three-year rotational initiative is specifically designed to prepare participants for leadership roles by immersing them in various departments across the organization for lengthy periods of time.

Participants of this program gain deep and diverse experience by working on real projects in functions, such as marketing, supply chain and finance, while receiving mentorship and training. This hands-on approach equips future leaders with a broad skill set and a deep understanding of the company's global operations, while building an internal "army of promotable giants."

## SHADOWING OPPORTUNITIES

Job shadowing is all about watching the legends at work. These opportunities let employees observe colleagues in different roles to gain a deeper understanding of their responsibilities. It's a great way to inspire growth, improve collaboration and help

# WORLD-CLASS CULTURES PROVIDE DEVELOPMENTAL SET LISTS WITH DIVERSE OPPORTUNITIES FOR GROWTH.

———

employees explore potential career paths within the organization.

### Etsy

Etsy, the online marketplace specializing in handmade and vintage products, has a self-directed shadow program. Employees can choose different departments they wish to shadow based on their interests or learning goals. Employees can participate in the program shortly after joining the company, with some starting as early as their first few months. The team member spends a day observing colleagues in different departments, receiving a behind-the-scenes look at how various teams contribute to the company's mission. This initiative fosters empathy, breaks down silos and encourages cross-departmental collaboration by deepening team members' understanding of the challenges and workflows of their peers.

### Wildbit

Wildbit, a small Philadelphia-based software company focused on team productivity tools, like Postmark and Beanstalk, takes job shadowing to another level, offering a unique program designed to deepen collaboration across its remote workforce. Their shadow program adapts to virtual environments by using tools that facilitate collaboration and communication across distances. Team members can "shadow" colleagues via video calls, screen-sharing sessions and collaborative platforms like Slack or Zoom, allowing them to study workflows, observe customer support interactions, join discussions and even work alongside their peers in real time, regardless of location. This approach fosters empathy, enhances understanding across departments and strengthens collaboration among a geographically dispersed team. So, no excuses if your company is a remote workforce.

## PEER-LED LEARNING

Sometimes, the best learning comes from your work colleagues. Peer-led learning initiatives encourage employees to share their knowledge and learn from one another. These sessions are collaborative and foster a culture of continuous learning while strengthening team dynamics and trust.

### Spotify

Music streaming service Spotify did just that and implemented peer-led "learning circles." These are informal groups in which team members come together to share their expertise and learn from each other on various topics such as coding, public speaking and creative problem-solving. These circles foster a collaborative learning environment, empowering employees to mentor one another in areas they are passionate about. This initiative encourages knowledge-sharing across the organization out of pure love of the collective whole and strengthens the company's culture of continuous learning and personal development.

WITH ANY of these developmental formats, you'll create a workplace where employees don't just perform—they thrive. The key is to offer diverse opportunities and support both personal and professional goals. You don't have to implement *all* of these programs, but you need to do *something* to keep the engagement going. So, ask yourself...

- Are you creating a stage where employees can shine?
- Do you have a formalized program through which your team members can grow?

If not, it's time to make some adjustments and start building the kind of culture where growth takes center stage. When you make this type of investment, your organization becomes a chart-topping hit, loved by employees and admired by everyone watching.

# GREATEST HITS

**1** **Make growth part of the gig**—Development isn't a perk; it's a promise. Rock stars don't stay relevant without evolving, and your employees shouldn't have to either.

**2** **Mix your learning formats**—Blend formats like mentoring, shadowing, cross-training and self-paced options to fit every style and grow top talent.

**3** **Create promotable giants**—Help employees develop beyond their job descriptions. When you invest in both personal and professional growth, you sharpen talent and build loyalty.

I think what's important
is to communicate.
If people don't know
what's going on, they'll
make it up.

**JOAN JETT**

# COMMUNICATE LIKE CRAZY

T HE ESSENCE of any thriving company culture boils down to one fundamental truth: People want to feel connected. Employees yearn to have a voice, to be heard and to be in the know. Without a strong communication framework, the best ideas are never shared, innovation stalls and employees begin to feel like they're just another cog in the machine. But when communication flows like a perfectly curated playlist, magic happens.

This chapter is all about mastering the art of over-communication—because when you communicate like crazy, you create an engaged, motivated and aligned workforce.

## THE POWER OF AN EMPLOYEE'S VOICE

Imagine this: A company rolls out a shiny new policy, and everyone finds out about it through the grapevine. What's the immediate reaction? Confusion, skepticism and a sense of exclusion. Employees don't just want to *know* what's happening; they want to *feel* like they're a part of it.

### Best Buy

Take a note from electronics retailer Best Buy. They implemented a biweekly "Employee Voice" video series, where team members submitted ideas and questions via videos from their phones. Leadership would then answer these in short, snappy videos shared company-wide. This initiative not only amplified employee voices but also gave a transparent look into decision-making.

IF YOU'RE THINKING, "Sounds great, but where do I start?" don't worry. I've got you covered with ten formats (and some brand examples in each area) you can use to develop a communications songbook. Are you ready to get the creative communication juices flowing?

## #1—PRINT

Traditional print might seem old school, and your brand may be averse to "killing trees," but this medium is still effective for reaching employees who prefer tactile communication. Whether it's posters in break rooms, branded postcards celebrating wins or quarterly magazines featuring employee stories, print collateral creates moments of pride. Print is tangible, and employees often appreciate the effort that goes into creating physical materials. This format works especially well for multi-generational teams.

### Marriott International

Hotel giant Marriott International places "employee spotlights" in their printed monthly newsletters. Each issue features stories of associates' milestones, creating a sense of belonging and recognition. These highlights often include work anniversaries, personal achievements and community-service contributions, reminding team members that they're valued beyond just their day-to-day roles. By showcasing diverse voices across departments and regions, Marriott reinforces its "people first" culture and strengthens pride in being part of a global hospitality brand.

## #2—VIDEO

Video is the closest thing to face-to-face communication. It's visual, emotional and deeply engaging. Consider recording updates from company executives, team-specific shout-outs or training modules. Videos bring energy and personality to otherwise static updates, allowing leadership to communicate authenticity and enthusiasm.

### Asana

Asana, a cloud-based project management company, created a "Team Wins" video series, where team leaders share weekly successes and updates, fostering a sense of accomplishment across the organization. These short clips highlight not only major milestones but also small, everyday victories that keep teams motivated. By making wins visible and shareable, Asana strengthens cross-team connection and reinforces a culture that celebrates progress, not just end results.

### Shopify

Showcased in the previous chapter for the company's self-directed education programs, Shopify launched "Morning Jams," which are short daily videos for employees, highlighting the company priorities for the day. These videos are infused with humor and personality, making them a must-watch for the team.

# #3—E-LEARNING

Communication isn't just about updates; it's about empowerment. Digital learning platforms allow employees to gain skills and knowledge at their own pace. E-learning tools can deliver updates alongside actionable content, ensuring employees are informed while also being equipped to grow. A warning when it comes to e-learning: Content alone isn't enough. Interactivity for participants is key.

## Nestlé

The sheer size of Nestlé, the world's largest food and beverage company, practically requires distance-based, digital communication; however, *how* they use it is what makes them stand out. Short video lessons and interactive challenges train employees on sustainability practices and encourage engagement at Nestlé.

## Walmart

Walmart also understands that the best e-learning content incorporates interactivity. The retail goliath uses e-learning modules to explain new safety protocols by gamifying the experience with quizzes and leaderboards. It's the perfect blend of edu-tainment.

## #4—TEXT

Not all companies are onboard with this one, but for real-time updates, SMS texts are unbeatable. This is the preferred method of communicating to today's younger generations. Whether it's sending shift reminders or sharing a quick "thank you," texts keep employees in the loop. Texting is particularly effective for teams that are always on the move or have limited access to computers. Old-school managers are just going to have to get past the idea that employees already have their phones on them at all times. Relevant brands will use texting to their advantage.

### Target

Walmart competitor Target uses text notifications for immediate feedback after team huddles, ensuring employees feel heard and acknowledged. Now *that* is real-time data from every interested team member. This instant loop not only spotlights concerns or suggestions quickly but also allows leaders to spot trends in engagement across stores. By acting on the feedback, Target demonstrates responsiveness, which strengthens trust and reinforces a culture of open communication.

## Domino's Pizza

Pizza delivery chain Domino's Pizza uses text campaigns to share fun challenges, like "Snap a Pic of Today's Best Teamwork Moment," an initiative designed to celebrate and recognize the value of teamwork within its workforce. This program encourages employees to capture and share moments where collaboration and team spirit are evident in their daily tasks and then rewards those participants with small prizes. Many companies use texting as customer-marketing campaigns, but think of all the possibilities of using it *internally* to engage employees.

## #5—ONE-ON-ONES

Nothing beats the personal touch of one-on-one meetings. Whether formal or informal, these interactions are where you truly connect and listen. One-on-ones build trust and alignment. For many employees, these moments define their relationship with the organization.

## REI

REI, an American retail and outdoor recreation services brand, introduced Trail Talks, which pair managers and employees for walking meetings, combining productivity with physical activity. On-point, branded employee engagement at its best.

### Trader Joe's

Trader Joe's, a favorite grocery store chain of urban Millennials and Gen Z, encourages its managers to schedule monthly 15-minute Coffee Chats with each team member. These informal check-ins build rapport and uncover valuable insights. Focused time with the boss in a one-on-one setting is one of the greatest retention strategies for today's workforce.

### Brian Washburn

During his tenure at Tampa International Airport as senior manager of airfield operations, Brian Washburn took one-on-ones to the next level by implementing a unique leadership approach he had learned from his time in the Coast Guard, called Tri-P—a three-way, in-person discussion with two other managers to work through critical project planning or airport policies. In this case, the forum was one-on-one-on-one.

Decision discussions between the participants— many times with differing opinions—were imperative for collective buy-in, to purposefully challenge the status quo and to work through obstacles in airport processes. Getting three leaders physically together was always tough, but Brian knew that these forums would foster open discussion, trust-building and consistency in processes. And Tampa's airport operations are better because of it.

## #6—EMPLOYEE SURVEYS

Surveys are the ultimate two-way communication tool. They're your chance to listen (at scale)—and act on what you hear. Regular, targeted surveys can help identify pain points, uncover opportunities and give employees a sense of connection to the band.

### Cleveland Clinic

One of the most well-known and innovative US medical centers, Cleveland Clinic implemented what they call Pulse Surveys. Like the name suggests, these regular surveys take the pulse (pun intended) of the clinic's workforce to collect real-time feedback. Contrary to the massive, one-time, annual employee survey most companies employ, Cleveland Clinic distributes Pulse Surveys every two weeks to all staff members, asking questions like, "What's one thing we could improve?" Simple and straightforward by design, the surveys glean results that help guide leadership in real time.

### Etsy

Etsy implemented Innovation Feedback Loops as one of their many employee engagement initiatives. Innovation Feedback Loops are short electronic surveys that ask team members for creative solutions to specific challenges. These internally crowd-sourced surveys foster a culture of innovation while positively influencing associates to stick around.

## #7—DIGITAL NEWSLETTERS

Weekly or monthly newsletters keep employees in the loop without overwhelming them. Because printed newsletters have gone the way of classic rock stations—both of them extremely rare these days— the focus may be on creating a robust digital format. Digital newsletters are a fantastic way to centralize updates and inject creativity into communication. And once in place, they can be regularly produced and distributed across the entire enterprise. To create more interest than simple text on the screen, add in some multimedia elements like videos, GIFs or even QR codes that lead to more information.

# WHEN YOU COMMUNICATE LIKE CRAZY, YOU CREATE AN ENGAGED, MOTIVATED AND ALIGNED WORKFORCE.

———

### HubSpot

HubSpot kicks off its newsletters with a Spotify playlist that is completely curated by employees. That simple element sets the tone for the week's priorities. The playlists reflect the personality and diversity of the workforce, giving team members a way to contribute creatively outside their core roles. It's a lighthearted touch that reinforces belonging and reminds employees their voices shape not just the business but the culture too.

### Mailchimp

Email and marketing automation platform Mailchimp includes interactive "Trivia Breaks" in their newsletters, where employees can answer fun questions and win small prizes while staying informed. The trivia not only reinforces company updates in a playful way but also sparks friendly competition across teams. By blending recognition with lighthearted engagement, Mailchimp turns a routine newsletter into something employees actually look forward to reading.

# #8—SOCIAL MEDIA

Most people think of social media as external-facing, but I'm referring to internal social platforms. Company intranets and private social sites create dynamic hubs for communication. Organizations can use them for sharing updates, celebrating wins or sparking conversations.

## Buffer

Buffer, a fully remote social-media marketing and management platform, leverages a private feed on X (formerly Twitter) to inform its employees about company updates in an informal, relatable style. This approach mirrors the very platforms Buffer helps clients manage, making communications feel authentic and on-brand. By meeting employees where they already spend time online, Buffer keeps its distributed workforce aligned while maintaining a sense of transparency and cultural consistency across time zones.

## Coca-Cola

Coca-Cola uses Workplace by Facebook to post daily "High Five" stories celebrating the rock stars who exemplify the brand's core values. The program turns recognition into a shared, social moment—visible not just to managers but also to peers across the organization. By weaving recognition into everyday communication, Coca-Cola reinforces its culture of appreciation while creating a steady stream of positivity that keeps employees connected and motivated. Simple, but effective.

## #9—POLLS

Quick polls, especially ones that use technology, are an easy way to gauge employee sentiment. They can break the monotony of communication while still delivering actionable insights. Bonus points if you make them fun and interactive.

### Sweetgreen

The fast-casual salad concept Sweetgreen uses its intranet to feature weekly polls with multiple-choice questions like, "What's your favorite seasonal salad ingredient?" You might think questions like this are a waste of team members' time, but quick, playful polls lead to serious engagement when used for strategic decisions like menu changes.

### Adobe

Computer software giant Adobe uses quick polls during team meetings to gather feedback on new initiatives, ensuring that every voice is considered. Text polling products like Poll Everywhere are fun and engaging, since participants use their own cell phones and the accumulated results are both immediate and anonymous.

## #10—TOWN HALLS

Quarterly or monthly "town hall" meetings are great for big-picture updates. These are more interactive than all-staff meetings. As the name suggests, these are Q&A opportunities that help everyone better understand the company's business. Some companies are now employing video live streams for remote teams to be actively involved. These forums clarify vision, align teams and foster transparency.

### Canva

Online graphic design platform Canva holds "Creative Vision" town halls, where employees can pitch ideas live to leadership, blending inspiration with practicality. These direct-voice sessions give team members an opportunity to shape future tools, features and workplace initiatives, reinforcing the company's open and innovative culture. By spotlighting employee-driven creativity in front of decision makers, Canva ensures great ideas don't get lost in silos and that innovation truly comes from every level of the organization.

### Procter & Gamble

Procter & Gamble's town halls also include live question-and-answer sessions, but they are facilitated by a charismatic host. This internal host helps frame tough topics in a constructive way, encourages diverse voices and keeps the energy level high throughout the session. P&G's approach transforms what could be routine corporate updates into authentic conversations, building transparency and trust between leadership and employees.

## COMMUNICATE THE WAY THEY WANT

Today's workforce is diverse—more than ever before. Some employees are tech wizards glued to their smartphones, while others prefer old-school print or face-to-face interactions. Communication isn't one-size-fits-all; it's about meeting people where they are. In every way possible, we should try to communicate with our employees in the language in which they dream. Multilingual, multimedia and multitasking—that's the trifecta.

## FedEx

FedEx created an internal podcast for employees to listen to during commutes. It covers company updates and fun trivia. By packaging important messages in a conversational, on-the-go format, FedEx meets employees where they are and makes staying informed effortless. The inclusion of lighthearted content alongside serious updates also humanizes leadership, making the company's culture feel more approachable and connected. It's proof that communication doesn't have to feel like work.

## Alorica

Customer experience solutions company Alorica launched its innovative Speak Your Language program as part of its commitment to inclusivity. It leverages real-time language translation tools and multilingual training materials to ensure employees feel valued and understood. By translating newsletters, videos and even live conversations into multiple languages, Alorica not only boosted employee satisfaction but also enhanced cross-team collaboration across its diverse workforce.

### Hard Rock International

I grew up on comic books. So, when I took over as head of training and development for Hard Rock, I took a cue from my childhood and converted all of the printed training materials into visual picture books. Instead of teaching a new busser how to clean, clear and set a table—which could easily be done with a single page of text information in a manual—I opted for creating a series of comic book–like photo pages of a busser visually performing these functions. Other than short text captions displayed underneath some photos, we used very few words. What would have been an inexpensive single page became six costlier visual pages. But the benefits: They assisted people with dyslexia and learning disabilities, they reduced or eliminated the need for language translations, and they provided crystal clear and consistent direction on how to do the job. Think about LEGO or IKEA furniture instructions, or even airline safety cards. There are

# TO TAP INTO TODAY'S WORKFORCE, COMMUNICATE TO EMPLOYEES IN THE LANGUAGE IN WHICH THEY DREAM.

———

no words in these amazing communication tools, yet everyone knows exactly what to do. Speaking in the language that people dream in *is* engagement.

## AS IF YOUR CULTURE DEPENDS ON IT

Communication is the lifeblood of your culture. That's why leaders can't afford to leave communication to chance—because in the absence of clarity, employees will fill the silence with their own version of the story.

When you communicate like crazy, employees aren't just informed—they're inspired, engaged and ready to bring their best selves to work. So, grab your mic, turn up the volume and start creating those epic communication moments that will take your culture to the next level.

## GREATEST HITS

1 **Give employees the mic—**
Make communication a two-way street
by giving your team a voice, not just a
one-directional memo. Listening builds
buy-in and sparks innovation.

2 **Use every communication channel—**
Tap into every format at your disposal (video,
print, texts, one-on-ones) to apply your
messaging to every preference and ensure
it lands.

3 **Speak the language (that people dream in)—**
From podcasts to comic books to
multilingual tools, tailor communication
so clearly and creatively that everyone
understands and embraces the messaging.

The people have the power. All we have to do is awaken the power in the people.

**PATTI SMITH**

# EMOTIONALLY CONNECT THEM TO THE GIG

I F YOU want employees to show up energized, engaged and ready to crush it, you've got to do more than just provide a paycheck. Employees need to be emotionally connected to their role, their team and your organization. Without that connection, they're just clocking in and out. They're not "all-in," bringing their best selves to the gig. And that's bad for business, bad for culture and bad for the future of your company.

Think of your company as a band. If your employees don't feel like they're playing an integral part of the music, then all you've got is noise. But when they're dialed in, emotionally connected and tuned to the same purpose, you create an unforgettable performance that fans (your customers) will never forget.

So, how do we connect them to the gig?

## MAKE IT WORTH THEIR TIME

Your employees are walking, talking ambassadors of your brand. But here's the kicker: They won't represent it authentically if their day-to-day experience doesn't align with the company's purpose and culture.

Think about the last time you were 100 percent invested in something. You gave it your time, your energy and even your after-hours brainpower because it mattered to you. That's what we want for our employees... but we have to earn it. For employees to stick around, they need to believe their job is worth their time and attention—both at work and away from it. When they're home, they should feel good about their contributions, not drained by a toxic environment or disengaged from boring tasks.

This starts by showing them how their work makes a difference. People crave meaning. Show them how their efforts drive the company's purpose, affect customers and contribute to a bigger mission... and they will become brand ambassadors for the company. Bruce Springsteen once said, "The best music is essentially there to provide you something to face the world with." The sentiment is true for work. When employees see the larger story they're helping to tell, they bring more passion, creativity and energy to the gig.

### Palmetto Hospitality Group

The leadership at Palmetto Hospitality Group, a boutique hotel management company, implemented Guest Story Sessions, where employees share how their specific efforts created memorable guest experiences. These jam sessions are a celebratory opportunity for employees to reflect on the tangible impact their positive work has on the guests, with the obvious outcome that the team members leave the sessions feeling proud of the roles they play.

### Zappos

Cultural icon Zappos uses a unique and highly influential tool that embodies the company's soul and core values: the Culture Book. It was created to reinforce Zappos's commitment to fostering a strong, authentic workplace culture that aligns with their mission to deliver their exceptional "WOW" customer service ... but it has become so much more.

The Culture Book is a collection of unfiltered, employee-written reflections about working at Zappos. Every year, employees are invited to contribute their thoughts on what the Zappos culture means to them; the unedited entries are then compiled into a printed book. It has become such a big part of the company's lore that other brands and industries study its cultural significance. Zappos's Culture Book isn't just a document; it's a powerful tool for alignment, storytelling and connection.

WHEN YOU can give everyone on the team an unfiltered voice and a secured spot in the company's legacy, the employee engagement (if I can channel my inner Spinal Tap) "goes to eleven"—and team members become brand ambassadors.

**Is a Culture Book something your company could implement? Because this best practice seems too undeniable to ignore.**

## MINDSET: THE FOUNDATION FOR CONNECTION

You can't build lasting emotional engagement without tackling mindset. Leaders *must* approach this employee "need" with intention, creating an environment where team members feel respected, valued and invested.

In case you are wondering how to influence an employee's mindset, there are a couple of ways.

First, you can foster an open-door culture where employees share ideas and concerns. Specifically, spend time in regular team discussions that align your people with the company's mission. Skip the corporate jargon and focus on stories, visuals and dialogue that make your culture come alive.

Then, you can set an example by living the brand's values every day. Specifically, discuss the values in team meetings and how they present themselves in the business. Perhaps you can display the company's values—via poster or wallet cards—and refer to them when big decisions are being made. When leadership walks the talk, employees are more likely to align their own mindset with the company's.

## Zingerman's Community of Businesses

At Zingerman's Community of Businesses, a group of small food-related companies based in Ann Arbor, Michigan, leadership promotes a "bottom-line change" philosophy. Managers regularly host open forums where employees voice concerns, share ideas and participate in decisions about company strategy. The leaders at Zingerman's live by an "open book finance" philosophy, where they share the financials of the business with team members. It's like giving every band member a say in creating the set list—ensuring everyone is along for the ride and fully invested in the performance. This transparency and collaboration create a strong sense of ownership and respect among employees, aligning their mindset with the company's mission of exceptional service and community impact.

### Findsome & Winmore

Findsome & Winmore, an Orlando-based marketing agency, emphasizes internal culture and teamwork. The cheekily named company has earned recognition for its commitment to creating a vibrant workplace environment, with a focus on values such as flexibility, collaboration and creativity. But a big part of their internal success is a result of quarterly "family meals" their team members enjoy. Shared, authentic team-building activities like potluck meals are designed to strengthen relationships, enhance the overall office experience and make each team member feel like part of a collective mission. Having personally worked with (and enjoyed a family meal with) the rock stars at Findsome & Winmore, I can attest that this is an engaged team.

# TO ENHANCE ENGAGEMENT, LET EVERY EMPLOYEE SHOWCASE THEIR TALENT WHILE CONTRIBUTING TO THE OVERALL SOUND.

———

### Deion Sanders

Pro football legend Deion Sanders has dramatically reshaped the culture of the Colorado Buffaloes football program with his leadership style as head coach, emphasizing personal development, accountability and excellence. When he arrived in 2023, the University of Colorado was one of the weakest teams in their conference, but "Coach Prime" Sanders brought a transformative vision to the team. Fostering a winning mentality and leveraging his reputation as an NFL icon, he attracted elite recruits, significantly raised the program's visibility and reinvigorated the fan base. But that's not what makes this example special.

Sanders' approach goes beyond the field and focuses on molding players into responsible men, making his leadership resonate deeply with each one of them. His mindset and infectious approach changes everything when players feel respected, valued and invested. Sure, the amazing results include packed stadiums, record TV ratings and a sense of optimism not seen in years—marking a revival of the team's on-field performance and the surrounding community's spirit—but touching the hearts of men is perhaps the greatest game Sanders has ever played. Well done, Coach.

## DEFINE YOUR ORGANIZATIONAL PILLARS

I subscribe to the belief that company culture is really just a collection of humans who exhibit shared, learned behaviors—good or bad—which, over time, create a known "personality." But to create the "shared" part, you *have* to define what you want those behaviors to be. If you don't define your culture, someone else will. And trust me, it won't be pretty. Or even close to what you want.

The backbone of emotional connection is a clearly defined culture that resonates with your employees. When people know what you stand for—your mission, purpose and values—they can decide if they want to stand with you. I could write a book on this (I did) and I could teach a class on this (I do), but to truncate all of it for you, start by answering these questions:

- What's the "why" behind our business?
- What do we believe as a company?
- How does our culture feel in action?
- What operating guidelines do we need in place?
- What specific outcomes would prove that our values exist?

Once all of these questions (and more) are answered and the organizational pillars of the brand are fleshed out, communicate it all in a way that sticks. Make it a constant drumbeat in your onboarding, team meetings and daily operations.

### GreenSpark Energy

At GreenSpark Energy, a renewable energy company, employees receive free solar panel installation for their homes. This program reflects the brand's commitment to sustainability and ensures that team members don't just promote the values—they live them every day. It's the quintessential example of a product that is so good that the employees are also proud customers. They're brand ambassadors—on and off the clock.

### SodaStream

SodaStream, a global manufacturer of home carbonation systems, is known for its emphasis on corporate values, sustainability and fostering a unique company culture. The company's "Values" video, shown during employee orientations, is a key tool in introducing new hires to the brand's ethos, goals and expectations. Unlike traditional employee handbooks or wallet cards, this video is designed to communicate SodaStream's core values in an engaging and memorable way.

What's unique about this "corporate" video is the use of humor, impactful graphics, storytelling and simplicity, which all come together in a fantastic way to reinforce the core values: sustainability, innovation, social responsibility and fun. By showing this video on Day 1 during orientations, SodaStream ensures that new employees start their journey with a strong understanding of the company's values while instilling a sense of belonging and pride in being part of a purpose-driven organization.

## Life's Food

Life's Food, a family-owned Carolinas-based franchisee of 26 Five Guys restaurants, made a bold move in 2014 by incorporating a faith-based approach into the business. We have forever been told to keep church and state separate, yet when the franchise owners realized that crew members were bringing their whole selves to the job—the good, the bad and the ugly—they reflected on their personal values, took a page from the Bible and made a cognizant decision to serve the needs of the people... albeit in an unorthodox way.

To be clear, the owners weren't interested in forcing Bible-study groups or pre-shift prayers on the crew members. Rather, they recognized that many on the team struggled with basic human needs—physical, emotional and, yes, spiritual—and decided to lead with faith.

Before you get too freaked out, check out the innovative initiatives the company introduced:

- **Workplace chaplains**—What started out as a chaplain friend of the owners attending an all-hands meeting as a resource for team members to work through personal issues has become a permission-based group of counselors who make weekly rounds to each location to interface with the crew. The voluntary interactions can include everything from prayer and biblical discussions to dealing with substance abuse, the loss of a loved one or thoughts of depression and suicide.

- **MyChap app**—As part of the chaplaincy program, the company offered crew members a free app to download on their phones that gives access to a chaplain at any time, any day, for a phone call, Zoom meeting or in-person offsite meetup. Although the owners' personal cell phone numbers are posted on the restaurants' back-of-the-house walls for authentic open communication, employees use the MyChap app to anonymously work through life's issues with their trusted chaplain partners.

- **Caring teams**—With the help of an outside Christian-based organization, each restaurant created an internal group of brand ambassadors called a Caring Team. These teams became decentralized decision-making for crew members in need. With a budget, structure and identified guidelines, Caring Teams assist crew members with financial loans, moving, getting their brakes fixed, transportation issues and even homelessness. Once the program guidelines are established, Caring Teams make decisions without ownership involvement or direct approval.

This is the greatest employee assistance program I've ever seen. And one that actually gets used. These initiatives transcend any specific religion and are available to every crew member. Life's Food's gutsy approach is certainly *not* for every organization, and the owners weren't even sure how all of this would be received. But the overwhelmingly positive responses and nonstop "thank you"s from the majority of the crew members after that first meeting validated their beliefs. And, as a by-product, strengthened the company's business results.

Since these revolutionary initiatives, Life's Food's employee turnover has consistently dropped over the last decade, and the company now boasts 50 percent less turnover than the industry's average. Employee turnover is the root of so many financial woes in the restaurant industry, so believe me when I say that high employee retention in *this* industry is a game changer.

I could spend even more time sharing the company's stellar benefits—like cash bonuses for crew members or company cars for general managers—but I believe it's Life's Food's faith-based business approach that has positioned the brand to be certified on the "Great Places to Work" list three years in a row and counting. Employee engagement flourishes here.

### One Village Coffee

When new employees join One Village Coffee, a small roaster with a focus on social impact, their introduction to the company doesn't start with paperwork or policies—it begins with an immersive experience that ties them directly to the company's mission of sustainability, fair trade and community impact. This onboarding initiative, called "The Journey

# EMOTIONALLY CONNECT EMPLOYEES TO THE GIG AND YOU BUILD A COMMUNITY OF BRAND ADVOCATES.

———

Begins," is hands-on, inspiring and deeply connected to the company's purpose and values.

Want to see the greatest onboarding process designed to emotionally connect people to a brand? Get ready to have your mind blown. Check out what "The Journey Begins" offers:

- Employees start their onboarding by learning about the journey of coffee beans—from the farms where they're grown to the final cup in a customer's hand.

- The new hires then participate in virtual or in-person "meet the grower" sessions, where they hear directly from farmers in partner communities. This gives them a firsthand understanding of the fair-trade practices the brand champions and how their work connects to supporting global sustainability and small-scale farmers.

- Employees are then brought to the company's roastery, where, guided by experienced team members, new employees help roast a batch of coffee, learning how temperature, timing and technique affect the flavor profile. They also get hands-on training in cupping (tasting and evaluating coffee) to better understand the company's commitment to quality.

- New team members then gather for a storytelling session led by senior leaders, where they learn about the company's history, mission and values. In these sessions, employees are encouraged to share what drew them to the company, creating a two-way dialogue. At the end of the session, they write a personal "impact statement," reflecting on how they hope to contribute to the company's purpose.

- Next, new employees spend a day volunteering with a local nonprofit organization aligned with the company's mission, such as a food bank or an environmental conservation group. This reinforces the company's belief in giving back and is meant to make employees feel that they're contributing to something bigger than just coffee.

- Finally, the program culminates in a team-wide gathering called "Welcome to the Village." This casual, celebratory event brings together existing and new employees to share a meal, swap stories and strengthen their sense of belonging. Each new team member receives a custom coffee mug engraved with the company's mission and their start date—a token symbolizing their role in the larger community.

I mean... wow!

There is no doubt every single team member at One Village Coffee knows exactly how their role is uniquely (and collectively) creating positive global change. Inspiring, isn't it?

WHEN YOU emotionally connect employees to the gig—to their role, their team and the organization—you create something far greater than a job; you build a community of passionate advocates. Like the innovative brands I shared here, set up the conditions so your employees *feel* it, *own* it and *live* it every day. That's how you rock not just your culture but also your results.

# GREATEST HITS

1 **Help employees find meaning in the mission**—When the job becomes bigger than a paycheck and team members see how their efforts make a difference, they shift from clocking in to buying in.

2 **Make mindset the main focus**—Lead with intention, model the values and create space for open conversations that align hearts and heads with the culture.

3 **Bake purpose into the employee journey**—From onboarding to team rituals, infuse every moment with meaning so people feel proud of where they work and who they work with.

It's stardom to be
in the company of
people you admire.

**BONO (U2)**

# 9

# TREAT THEM LIKE ROCK ROYALTY

A S WE discussed way back in chapter 4, it's an employee's world now. They hold all the power. And they expect a lot from an employer.

In today's competitive landscape, employees aren't just looking for a paycheck—they're searching for purpose, acknowledgment and a sense of belonging. Originally reported by workplace platform Socialcast in 2016, multiple subsequent studies over the last decade—including by Gallup, OC Tanner, Apollo Technical and Vantage Circle—have all confirmed that 69 percent of employees would work harder if they felt their efforts were better appreciated. Additionally, the Society of Human Resource Management's insights in 2023 on "Building a Connected Workforce" tout that companies with strong recognition programs see 31 percent lower turnover rates. The truth is, when employees feel valued, they're not just satisfied—they're inspired.

To keep the talent in your band, you've got to roll out the red carpet and treat your team like rock royalty.

This chapter dives into creative and impactful ways to make employees feel like VIPs. From unique incentives to personalized perks, these initiatives will show your people they're the main attraction of your organization. Let's talk about the various ways to do that.

## UNIQUE INCENTIVE PROGRAMS

When it comes to incentives, the days of generic gift cards or a company logo hat are over. Employees want rewards that resonate with their individuality and achievements.

### BetterUp

BetterUp, a personal coaching platform, offers employees experiential rewards, such as personalized coaching sessions and VIP access to exclusive events, like their Uplift Summit—a high-profile, celebrity-filled thought leadership gathering traditionally targeted for external executive audiences. These programs go beyond monetary compensation, creating experiences that deepen loyalty.

## Brooklyn Brewery

Another standout is Brooklyn Brewery, which gives its employees unique incentives like tickets to exclusive beer festivals and brewing workshops for achieving team goals. It's not just about the reward—it's about creating moments that celebrate success in meaningful ways.

## Recology

Recology, a San Francisco–based waste management and recycling company, is a 100 percent employee-owned company through its stock ownership plan. Fully funded by the company, this retirement benefit plan provides team members with shares of the company over time so they become co-owners. As you can imagine, employee ownership fosters many positive outcomes—innovation, efficiency, teamwork, accountability, mission alignment—but imagine how much more motivated and engaged employees are because they directly benefit from the company's profitability. This incentive has significantly contributed to Recology's growth and success over the decades.

## SPOTLIGHT ON EXCELLENCE

Recognition is the standing ovation employees crave. It's one thing to say "thank you," but truly recognizing someone's contributions—publicly or privately—creates a lasting impression. As Freddie Mercury put it, "You can be the best singer in the world, but if the band doesn't work together, it won't matter."

Whether through annual awards or spontaneous acknowledgments, shining a spotlight on contributions inspires everyone to step up their game. If it makes sense for the brand, you could opt for tangible rewards like certificates, pins or badges, but the goal is for team members to *feel* valued. That's how to increase engagement. In fact, a 2022 Gallup article focused on bridging the generational gaps through recognition revealed that employees who receive regular recognition are four times more likely to be engaged. Four times!

### Caribou Coffee

Caribou Coffee is great at rewarding excellence. The brand offers employees adventure-based incentives, such as outdoor excursions, for meeting performance goals. A perfect reward for a wilderness-themed coffee

# TO KEEP TALENT IN YOUR BAND, YOU'VE GOT TO ROLL OUT THE RED CARPET AND TREAT THEM LIKE ROCK ROYALTY.

———

brand, and a true nod to a team member's exceptional contribution.

### Rackspace

The team at Rackspace Technology, a leading cloud computing and hosting company, pride themselves on providing excellence in every area. One of the highest honors a "Racker" can receive is the Fanatical Jacket Award, a recognition program that celebrates employees who go above and beyond in their work, aligning with the company's ethos of providing "fanatical experiences" to customers. As part of that recognition, recipients are awarded a custom leather jacket emblazoned with the Rackspace logo, signifying their iconic status as a standout contributor to the company's success.

### Taylor Swift

The biggest musical artist on the planet at the time of this writing, Taylor Swift made headlines for her extraordinary gratitude toward her tour truck drivers during her Eras Tour in 2024. In the middle of the tour, she awarded each truck driver a mind-blowing $100,000 cash bonus. For many of the drivers, this money provided opportunities that wouldn't normally be possible with their typical wages—making a sizeable down payment on a home or paying in full for college tuition. Additionally, Taylor wrote a handwritten letter to each driver, sealed with her branded monogram, emphasizing her appreciation for their hard work.

The life-changing combo of the bonus and the personalized letter showed Taylor's immense generosity and acknowledged the sacrifices these workers make, such as being away from their families for extended periods of time and enduring grueling schedules on the road. I assure you, these truck drivers are never leaving Taylor.

Perhaps this example seems unrelatable to you, especially from the highest grossing tour in history, which ultimately generated $2.2 billion dollars, but appreciating team members for their worth in any business solidifies loyalty. Regardless of the company's size, whether it's one person or the biggest in the industry—Taylor Swift happens to be both— spotlighting excellence amps up engagement. If you treat your employees the way Taylor does, trust me— they'll stay, stay, stay.

## TAILORED PERKS

As we touched on in chapter 3, one-size-fits-all doesn't work when it comes to benefits. Offering customized perks that align with your employees' lives shows that you care about their well-being, both on and off the job.

### Burton Snowboards

Burton Snowboards sets the bar with extras like season ski passes, on-site yoga classes and financial support for sustainable living practices. These tailored perks make perfect sense to their workforce. By weaving lifestyle benefits into the employee experience, Burton not only fuels passion for the outdoors but also reinforces its identity as a purpose-driven brand. The result is a culture where employees feel personally connected to the company's mission, both on and off the slopes.

### The Grommet

The Grommet, a company that helps launch innovative products, provides Passion Hours, where employees are given a few hours each week to work on personal projects or interests that inspire them. Whether it's exploring a new skill, volunteering or starting a side hustle, this customized benefit reinforces the company's belief in fostering creativity and individuality. How cool is that?

This tailored approach is designed to nurture employee well-being, and the Grommet has found that it often sparks innovative ideas from team members that benefit the business. Think about that: an innovative products company that fosters employees' personal innovation... to inspire *more* innovation. Brilliant!

## PEER-TO-PEER LOVE

Sometimes, the best recognition comes from within the band. Peer-to-peer programs encourage employees to recognize and celebrate each other's efforts, creating a sense of camaraderie and trust.

### Quick Quack Car Wash

California-based Quick Quack Car Wash, known for their customer-friendly membership options and commitment to sustainable practices, integrates peer-to-peer recognition into their company culture in two ways. One is through internal digital platforms and shared recognition boards, where employee recognitions are made visible to others in the organization, fostering motivation and engagement. Another way is by giving employees small budgets with which to reward their peers, making the recognition tangible and more meaningful.

### Southwest Airlines

Southwest Airlines has a robust peer-to-peer recognition program called Winning Spirit. Employees nominate peers who go above and beyond their roles and in demonstrating the company's core values. Winners receive recognition in corporate communications, along with tangible rewards such as points that can be redeemed for merchandise or travel benefits. This low-cost, on-brand program reinforces a sense of community and appreciation among co-workers.

### Hard Rock International

Some of the greatest programs my team and I created at Hard Rock were peer-to-peer recognitions that, once we implemented them, took on a life of their own and required no supervision or management involvement. Here are two of my faves:

- **"You Rock" pads**—These small blocks of adhesive paper provided space for one employee to recognize another for exemplary work or living the brand values, letting them know they "rocked." Filled-in sheets were then ripped off the pad and posted in the back-of-the-house halls or on employee breakroom walls. Some location managers collected these monthly and used them to help award employees-of-the-month.

- **The Golden Elvis**—This was a corporate support-center initiative in which we anonymously placed an 18-inch gold statue of the King (Elvis Presley) on the desk of an office employee who exceeded expectations in representing the brand's values. Accompanying the statue was a letter that explained why they were receiving the "Golden Elvis" and that they could keep it displayed at their desk for the entire month... but that they then would have to anonymously identify another co-worker and stealthily award the statue to them.

## MAKE IT EXPERIENTIAL

Sometimes, the type of focus and energy we put into creating memorable experiences for our customers could easily be used to rock our employees. It's not just about the reward itself—it's about creating an experience that celebrates their success.

Because I wanted *Engagement That Rocks* to be a wealth of innovative suggestions, let me share some additional ideas, not listed so far, that would get your employees involved and enhance their engagement. Consider the following best practices to help you create unique experiences for your team members:

- **Go teambuilding**—Hold non-work-related events to build your team, such as go-carting, bowling or miniature golf.

- **Surprise and delight**—Seek out opportunities to throw a party for your employees, offer random discounts on specific brand items or solicit answers to trivia questions or company procedures in exchange for prizes, such as company-branded merchandise, gift cards or concert tickets.

- **Random acts of kindness**—Every once in a while, buy several $1 lotto tickets and hand them out to team members before or during a shift. If lotto tickets are not your thing, create your own "random act" that makes sense for your business.

# THE BEST RECOGNITION COMES FROM WITHIN THE BAND; PEER-TO-PEER ACKNOWLEDGMENT IS POWERFUL.

---

- **Surprise delivery**—Order up a surprise delivery of a type of food that makes sense for your brand (e.g., pizza, chicken wings, mini-burgers, hot pretzels, frozen drinks, cinnamon buns) or even have a food truck stop by once a month.

- **Invite family**—Foster an environment in which spouses and kids can be included; this could be at a company BBQ or dinner, an annual conference or a "Bring Your Kid to Work" day.

- **White elephant gifts**—Consider implementing the popular and hilarious secret gift exchange during the end-of-year holidays.

- **Suggestion box**—If you don't already have open dialogue sessions to solicit employee feedback, such as quality circle meetings, create a non-threatening, anonymous suggestion box to gather feedback—and then act on those ideas to make the company better.

- **Boss swap for leaders**—Implement a program in which executives and managers work in entry-level staff positions for a day (perhaps once per year or quarterly). Walking in the employees' shoes will help leaders develop humility… and is always fun for the employees, as well.

- **Movie night**—Host a team movie night, complete with popcorn and Twizzlers. My team at Hard Rock used to watch only "rockumentaries" to build our music knowledge and perfect our craft, but the best part was just hanging out together outside of work.

- **Group break**—Pick a specific slow time of the day to take a 15- to 20-minute break as a team. Have a collective cup of coffee, watch videos or play a game of pool.

- **Beer thirty**—This is risky and certainly *not* for every brand, but some edgier companies select a time at the end of the work week to stop business early and share cocktails as a group.

- **Book club**—Start a monthly book club and have the team collectively read a business book over the course of a month or two, then discuss and share insights together. *Ehem*... I might have an idea or two of some books that would work.

## THE RECOGNITION MOVEMENT

Recognition isn't just a feel-good practice; it's a smart business strategy. In a 2023 Deloitte blog titled

"Future of Total Rewards: Trends and Strategies," the organization revealed that companies with strong recognition programs are 12 times more likely to achieve strong business outcomes. Meanwhile, as Deloitte also learned in its 2017–2018 "Business Chemistry" survey, 85 percent of employees say recognition programs improve their sense of belonging and engagement at work. These two data points prove that strong recognition programs work.

However, creating a culture of acknowledgment isn't just about programs; it's also about mindset. When leaders take the time to genuinely connect, recognize and reward their team, they create an environment where employees feel valued.

Treat your employees like the headliners they are, and they'll keep delivering show-stopping performances. When you roll out the red carpet for your team, they'll never want to leave the stage.

# GREATEST HITS

1 **Appreciation fuels retention—**
Regular, authentic recognition keeps your
team energized, loyal and ready to perform
their best.

2 **Ditch the one-size-fits-all approach—**
Personalized perks and custom rewards
resonate more deeply and show your team
you truly know (and value) them.

3 **Create experiences, not just incentives—**
Whether it's a handwritten note, free ski
passes or unlimited PTO, make your team
feel like VIPs on and off the clock.

For me, success is being able to give back to your friends, your family, your community, those in need and the world entire.

**RICHIE SAMBORA (BON JOVI)**

# USE PHILANTHROPY AS THE AMPLIFIER

LOYALTY TO any single company seems to be a rarity these days. People "job hop" like Cher changes outfits during a show. Internally, employees of today constantly ask, "How does *this* work in *this* job specifically benefit me?" If things don't gel with their idea of a good quality of life—because of the pay, benefits, hours, environment, culture or leadership—then they have no problem moving on to greener pastures. Because they can.

Most of those workforce "requirements" are within a leader's direct control. So is fostering the company's "soul." Yep, I said it: soul.

Does your brand have a heart? Because today's generations insist on doing good whenever and however possible, which includes working for an organization that does. Part of amping up employee engagement is tapping into the key elements that drive the talent pool. And a critical element that validates that the company has a heart is philanthropy: helping others that are less fortunate.

In a world where consumers seek more than just a transaction and employees yearn for purpose beyond a paycheck, companies that champion philanthropy are setting the gold standard. Philanthropy isn't merely a charitable side hustle anymore; it's a core business strategy. If you're looking for ways to make your company irresistible to employees and customers alike, tapping into philanthropy is a fantastic way to rock engagement.

## PURPOSE BEYOND PROFIT

When employees feel connected to a company's mission, work becomes a calling. Philanthropy offers a powerful way to create that connection. This isn't just about writing checks—although donating a portion of the company's profits to a cause is amazing. I'm talking about rolling up our sleeves and making a real impact for others. Trust me when I say that your employees *crave* this.

### Delta Airlines

Delta Airlines takes employee engagement to the skies—literally. The company organizes "Force for Global Good" trips, where employees have participated in initiatives like building homes in underprivileged communities and providing disaster relief around the world. While improving lives in places like Ghana and India, these initiatives build a sense of pride and fulfillment among Delta's workforce. Employees walk away from these experiences feeling good about themselves and deeply connected to Delta as a company with heart—a vehicle for change.

## THE UNDENIABLE POWER OF DOING GOOD

Philanthropy is not a hard thing to do, either. In fact, it often doesn't even require money—just time and support.

Philanthropy can be anything from cleaning up a beach or river to organizing a recycling drive to working in a food bank—all of which can be facilitated on your company's own timeline. It can also rally around designated dates and causes. For example, your company's philanthropic initiatives could support putting on an Earth Day event each April or implementing breast cancer awareness initiatives in the fall. Maybe wrapping an initiative around the company's birthday would be a great way to give back. It just depends on what makes sense for your organization. There are literally thousands of deserving charities and causes that need assistance. They can be well-known, global opportunities or small, local causes... and each can potentially resonate with your team.

But the brand *must* do something. Giving back is expected.

## WHY PHILANTHROPY ROCKS YOUR BRAND

Think of your organization's philanthropic efforts like a band that plays for a cause—the audience isn't just there for the music; they're there for the mission. Philanthropy amplifies a company's purpose, creating a rallying cry for employees and customers alike. Melissa Etheridge captures it perfectly: "The more you choose love, the more love is in your life." Philanthropy is that love in action—it's how a company shares its light and amplifies engagement through giving. And when that light comes from within your organization, it not only draws people in—it keeps them in harmony with your mission.

When companies embed "giving back" into the fabric of who they are, they create a loyal following of brand ambassadors who feel like a part of something

# PHILANTHROPY AMPLIFIES A COMPANY'S PURPOSE, CREATING A RALLYING CRY FOR EMPLOYEES.

———

meaningful. Advocacy brands have figured this out, and it's why they're rocking their industries.

Following are a few reasons—some with quantifiable, positive business results—to engage the brand in philanthropy:

- **Philanthropy is great for the community and the environment**—Who doesn't see the value in recycling, beach/river/park cleanups, hunger relief, sustainable products or feeding and clothing the homeless?

- **It engages and galvanizes the entire organization around a powerful and worthwhile goal**—Teams solidify when the job is more than a paycheck.

- **It gives employees an emotional connection to the brand and their jobs**—People want to do meaningful work.

- **It increases employee morale**—Team members who do purposeful, meaningful work are happier.

- **It decreases employee turnover**—When team members are happy, they stick around longer.

- **It provides a differentiator that reinforces your brand's positioning with consumers**—More socially minded customers make purchasing decisions based on issues they care about.

* **It offers positive media and public relations opportunities**—This may be less a reason than a good by-product, but once the outside world discovers the good work a company does, the brand will get credit in the form of free advertising.

* **It provides opportunities to more deeply involve strategic partners**—Vendors become part of the culture, versus just financially supporting the company's regular business.

* **It levels the organizational hierarchy**—When voluntarily focusing on a cause to help others—no pay or requirement involved—everyone is equal; there are no titles or positional power when working side-by-side with a co-worker, boss or senior executive on a charitable cause. Philanthropy is one of the great equalizers.

## WHERE TO START

If you're ready to turn up the volume on philanthropy but don't know where to begin, start by tuning into your brand's values. Think of it like creating a set list for a concert—you've got to pick the songs that resonate the most with your audience. Begin by asking yourself some foundational questions: What specific causes align with your company's mission? How can your products, services or resources make a difference? And most importantly, how can you involve your employees (and customers) in the journey? The key is to start with authenticity. You don't need a massive budget or a global footprint—you just need heart and a plan. Here's how:

- **Define your cause**—Choose a cause that aligns authentically with your brand values. Patagonia's environmental focus, for instance, fits perfectly with their outdoor gear. Identify a specific charitable cause that will rally the team together for something bigger than the job.

- **Engage your team**—Involve employees in choosing causes and participating in initiatives. You might discover that someone within your ranks is going through something that would suggest aligning with a specific charity (they have a relative with cancer and so they want to support cancer research, for example). Or you might learn that someone is super passionate about a cause (urban wildlife rescue or children's literacy, just to name a couple).

# TO AMP UP ENGAGEMENT, IMPLEMENT AND SUPPORT A VOLUNTARY, EMPLOYEE-LED PHILANTHROPIC GROUP.

———

- **Start small but think big**—Just taking the group out to do a small activity (working in a food bank, cleaning a park, feeding the homeless, starting a canned food drive) would be a good, safe start, especially if a specific charity doesn't naturally make sense for your business. Eventually, seemingly small initiatives, like donating a percentage of sales to a local charity, can make a huge impact.

- **Communicate transparently**—Be clear with the team about your goals and outcomes. Authenticity is key to building trust.

- **Measure impact**—Track and share the results of your efforts to demonstrate that you're walking the talk.

## Hard Rock International

One method Hard Rock International uses to bring its purpose-driven values to life is through the Ambassador Program. This is a voluntary, employee-led philanthropy group that exists at each property and strives to make the local community a little bit better. Members of this group are completely engaged, getting involved in charitable causes because they *want* to, not because they *have* to. Ambassadors meet regularly and seek out no-cost opportunities to help their communities, many times rallying around a colleague who has fallen on hard times. For many Hard Rockers, the Ambassador Program elevates the job beyond slinging drinks and making burgers.

Seriously consider implementing a voluntary, employee-led philanthropic group, starting with these questions:

- Is there a local cause your employees wish to wrap their arms around?

- Does one of your team members have a personal connection to a particular cause?

Seeking out answers to these questions is time and energy well spent, because finding a way to make an impact beyond the scope of your day-to-day business could be the catalyst that revolutionizes your company's morale, productivity and long-term success.

## NO-BRAINER RATIONALE

To set up an employee-led, volunteer philanthropy group, follow this simple process:

- **Share your philanthropic thoughts and goals with your team members**—Use all-staff meetings, department meetings, postings in an employee area or any combination thereof.

- **Solicit an initial core group**—Select one member from each business function or department to represent the entire company or property.

- **Allow the group to determine its own structure**—Let the core group decide whether meetings are open to everyone in the company, just a select few from each department or only formal, elected officers.

- **Support the group's causes**—Encourage the volunteer-employees to identify the local causes and activities they would like the brand to support.

- **Support the group's ongoing needs, where possible**—Offer up potential resources like meeting space, T-shirts, food and beverages.

- **Get out of the way**—Allow the group to take on a life of its own; through passionate, committed employees, the process will manage itself.

If you'd rather not instill this type of formality, then just create an open forum in which team members can show up, voice their opinions and participate in something meaningful. Even *that* would be a great start.

Today's generations are looking to offer up their loyalty to those companies that are truly active in making their communities better.

**Do you think this is too grandiose a concept to apply to your organization?**

Ask any 19-year-old what they now look for in an organization, and some language around "giving back" or "doing the right thing" is likely to pop up. This is how Gen-Z (and Millennials) grew up, and they expect this to be common practice in businesses today.

Here are some standout examples of brands that are turning up the volume on giving back.

## Bombas Socks

Bombas Socks follows a similar philosophy to TOMS Shoes, pioneers in this area. They've built their entire brand around giving back, donating one pair of socks for every pair purchased. Until I heard about Bombas, I was unaware that socks are *the* most requested items of people experiencing homelessness. This is a perfect example of a brand using their product for good, and with direct relevance and impact. To date, they've donated over 100 million items to shelters and organizations supporting the homeless. The result? Bombas has turned a simple product into a movement, creating loyal customers who are just as invested in the mission as the company itself.

## Axum Coffee

Axum Coffee, a small chain based in my hometown of Winter Garden, Florida, donates 100 percent of its profits to charitable causes, including orphanages, education and clean water initiatives in Africa. That's right, every single dollar of profit—once the building lease and employees are paid—goes to helping others. Employees and guests alike know that every cup of coffee fuels a bigger purpose, which turns an ordinary cafe visit into an extraordinary experience. It's a big part of why I have written a portion of my books there.

## Tori Kelly

A philanthropic enabler of a different sort is soulful singer-songwriter Tori Kelly. She uses her platform to support various causes, from mental health awareness to providing aid to disaster-stricken areas. Soon after Tori's initial launch into stardom on *American Idol*, she released a single called "Fill a Heart," which she wrote for the "Child Hunger Ends Here" campaign by Conagra Foods and Feeding America. As part of that campaign, she performed at various venues across the United States in her Fill a Heart Tour, each time helping out at the city's food banks during the day before performing at night. How about that? Philanthropist by day, rock star by night. By aligning

# COMPANIES THAT GIVE BACK AS A CORE PART OF THEIR IDENTITY DON'T JUST STAND OUT— THEY THRIVE.

———

her artistry with advocacy, Tori Kelly is creating a legacy that goes far beyond music.

### Wildflower Bread Company

The Wildflower Bread Company, based in Arizona, is another standout. This bakery and cafe chain runs their Helpings Campaign, where proceeds from certain menu items go to local charities. By aligning its business with the communities it serves, Wildflower creates a strong emotional connection with its customers and employees. Affectionately known as "bread heads," the team members at Wildflower are some of the most giving people I know.

### Hard Rock International

One thing about Hard Rock that most people would not know is that its commitment to doing good is unwavering... even when it costs more. This is one of the key reasons why I stayed with the brand for so long. One of the company's mottos—since its inception in 1971 and way before the saying was popularized—is "Save the Planet." The brand's founders went to great lengths to ensure that everyone—employees and guests—would know how important it was to care for the planet and its inhabitants, including having the motto emblazoned on a wall of every property. That will keep you honest, right? I mean, it's pretty hard to have "Save the Planet" in big block letters hanging on the wall and then *not* actively work on saving the planet. Brand advocates everywhere would scream, "Liar, liar pants on fire!" if that were the case. This was a great example of value accountability. It forced us to walk the talk. And we're better because of it.

There are so many philanthropic initiatives, but here are just two that always stood out to me:

- **Events**—I cannot recall a single Hard Rock Cafe event, whether it was live music or something celebratory, that did not have a charitable component. It was rock and roll with a heart!

- **Collateral**—All of the company letterhead, business cards, marketing material and training manuals were produced on recycled paper and with soy ink. Ironically, this always costs more and was a pain in the butt to execute, but it was worth sticking to the brand values.

### Nate St. Pierre

I met Nate St. Pierre in a hotel lobby at a hospitality conference and knew from the moment we connected that we would be in each other's orbits forever... and philanthropy was the bridge. Nate has created many innovative philanthropic initiatives, but the ones that use the combined power of community and love are the ones that truly stand out. Check these out:

- **Love Bomb**—Long before the term "love bombing" became tied to someone showering affection on someone to manipulate them (gross!), Nate formalized the concept of the Love Bomb—crowd-sourced, collective love, which could literally change (or save) a life in just five minutes for free. Here's how it worked: Each week, Nate and his business partner, Jay, would scour the internet and their local community looking for one struggling person who needed a little support. Engaging his organic network of 5,000 members across 50 countries, Nate would organize the team of volunteers to collectively and simultaneously drop a Love Bomb on the unsuspecting recipient, letting them know how much they matter and that an entire community was throwing them positive vibes, prayers and love. Can you imagine what it must feel like to get hundreds (or even thousands) of messages via text, email, Facebook and voicemail—all at once—letting you know that you are loved? Life changing.

- **Love Drop**—Taking the concept of the Love Bomb to the next level, Love Drops required a bit more commitment, organization, processes and gifting... but the rewards were awe-inspiring for recipients. On a regular basis, Nate would again surf the internet in search of authentic individuals and families in dire need. Sometimes, a family just needed money to pay the rent or prevent a mortgage from staying in default. Other times, they needed Christmas gifts for the kids. Or a single mother needed to find a job. It ran the gambit from groceries for the week for one family to replacing a washer and dryer set for another. Marshalling the heart-centered community that he had curated, Nate would put the challenge out to donate an item or dollar amount to help fill the need. Not an easy task to manage—this was built before there were platforms like Patreon or GoFundMe. Once all the resources were accumulated, and completely unbeknownst to the recipients, Nate and Jay would personally drive (or fly) to present the gifts. Often, the non-monetary gifts were the most touching for everyone involved. I will never forget the time Nate "love dropped" a car to a family that desperately needed a vehicle. A lot of tears and memories were made by all that day.

## MAKE "GIVING BACK" CORE TO YOUR BRAND

Obviously, the huge takeaway in this chapter is that philanthropy is a business imperative. In fact, I believe philanthropy could be the secret weapon for some companies in amping up employee engagement. Companies that embrace giving back as a core part of their identity don't just stand out—they thrive.

Whether you're a global giant like Hard Rock or a local gem like Axum Coffee, the key is authenticity. Don't just give for the sake of PR. Consumers and employees can smell insincerity a mile away, so your giving *has* to come from a place of genuine care and commitment. Give because it's the right thing to do.

When your company aligns its actions with its values, the results are transformative. Employees are more engaged, customers are more loyal and the world becomes a better place. That's the power of using philanthropy as the amplifier.

## GREATEST HITS

**1** **Purpose hits harder than perks**—Employees crave meaning in their work and want to work for a brand that gives back and stands for something real. These mission-driven companies become magnets for top talent.

**2** **Philanthropy unites your team**—Doing good together levels the playing field, deepens connection and builds pride across every title and department.

**3** **Giving back is a business strategy**—When your company's values show up in action, engagement skyrockets, loyalty grows and the brand becomes unforgettable.

It's very fun to be
weird, and it's very
boring to be normal.

**P!NK**

# 11

# BE SERIOUS ABOUT HAVING FUN

L ET'S GET REAL—most people spend more of their waking hours at work than anywhere else. And if your workplace culture feels like a soul-sucking, eight-hour solo road trip with no radio instead of backstage VIP party, don't expect your employees to bring their best selves to the gig. Employees want to be part of something that lights them up, not grinds them down. They want energy, connection and an environment that feels alive. If you want rock star performance, you need to build a stage where people *want* to show up. That's why fun at work is a necessity.

Yep, I said it—fun. It's not a distraction. It's not a luxury. It's not what you "hope" your team squeezes in once a quarter at the company picnic. It's not forced fun or superficial perks like ping-pong tables that never get used. I'm talking about a deep-seated commitment to joy, surprise and employee-first experiences.

Fun is a strategic driver. It's a cultural amplifier. And when done right, it's one of the most powerful tools you've got for employee engagement, which ultimately leads to loyalty and retention.

In a world where burnout runs rampant and disengagement is at an all-time high—Gallup found in its 2023 *State of the Global Workforce* report that 59 percent of employees worldwide are "quiet quitting" (doing only the bare minimum)—building a culture that people enjoy is your competitive advantage. And if you can get your team to fall madly in love with the vibe of your workplace, they'll go from being clock-punchers to brand ambassadors. From part-time roadies to full-on headliners.

## FUN—AN EMOTIONAL TRIGGER

Let's get a little psychological here—because fun at work isn't just about a good time; it's about how people *feel.* Joy, laughter, spontaneity—these aren't just mood boosters. They're neurochemical performance enhancers. When people laugh or feel connected, they release dopamine and oxytocin—hormones that boost memory, learning, trust and belonging.

You want innovation? Collaboration? Problem-solving? Those things don't happen in stale, fear-driven environments. They happen in safe, vibrant environments where people feel free to be themselves. Fun is emotional glue for organizations. It bonds teams. It diffuses stress. It turns "work friends" into family. When companies invest in fun, they're investing in well-being. And in today's era of mental health burnout, it's not just a nice-to-have. It's life support for many brands.

## WHY FUN MATTERS (LIKE, REALLY MATTERS)

Still think fun is fluff? Or touchy-feely? Let's do the math.

- A 2024 Gallup blog post revealed that engaged teams show 21 percent greater profitability. Why? Because when people love what they do and where they do it, they show up stronger, work harder and stay longer.

- In 2024, McKinsey & Company reported that companies with strong organizational health delivered three times higher total shareholder returns compared to less healthy businesses.

- According to BrightHR's *It Pays to Play* report, 62 percent of employees who have fun at work take fewer sick days.

- In Haystack's 2025 blog post "Fun at Work Isn't Frivolous; It's Essential," the article highlights how fun reduces stress, enhances retention and boosts collaboration.

When employees look forward to coming to work—not just for the paycheck but for the people, the play and the pulse—you've built something extraordinary. Fun builds connection. It boosts creativity, loyalty and even mental health. It fosters community, breaks down silos and transforms your culture into something magnetic. It inspires brand love. It humanizes leadership. And it helps your company become a place where people don't just stay—they stay *engaged*.

Want to retain your best talent and attract more of it? Start by making work feel less like a funeral (unless that's your business) and more like a music festival. Steven Tyler nailed it when he said, "If you're not having fun, you're doing it wrong." That's as true for a sold-out arena as it is for a Monday morning staff meeting—because when people genuinely enjoy the experience, they bring more of themselves to the performance.

# IF YOU WANT ROCK STAR PERFORMANCE, BUILD A STAGE WHERE PEOPLE WANT TO SHOW UP.

———

## HOW TO AMPLIFY THE FUN

Making "fun" a part of the day-to-day business can be part of the overall consistency, creativity and willingness to prioritize people that you bring to engagement.

Here are some ways to inject fun into your workplace:

* **Make it a leadership priority**—It starts at the top. Managers and executives need to participate—not just approve from the sidelines. Leaders must *model* fun, *support* fun and *fund* fun. Make joy as measurable as performance. Laugh openly and create space for levity during meetings and product rollouts.

* **Design signature events**—Create rituals people talk about all year. Maybe it's an annual lip sync battle, an internal award show or monthly themed "Fun Fridays." Whatever you choose, brand it. Make it yours. Make it memorable.

* **Gamify the everyday**—Big events are great, but the everyday touches are where the moments really live. Build micro-moments into the everyday rhythm of your business. Think confetti GIFs in emails, humorous signage, surprise snack drops or

Spotify playlists crowd-sourced by your team. Turn meetings, training sessions or quarterly reviews into contests or team-based competitions. It's not about budget—it's about *intention.*

- **Make it a shared experience**—Get employees involved in designing fun. Rotate planning committees, host idea contests or run "culture jams" where teams co-create their own events. Shared ownership is what turns top-down fun into grassroots culture.

- **Celebrate loudly**—Go big on recognition. Recognize "wins" in public, creative and even ridiculous ways. Costumes, surprise DJ sets, whatever gets the crowd going.

- **Break the routine**—Random themed days, spontaneous dance parties or impromptu karaoke in the breakroom shake things up and keep energy high.

- **Personalize the experience**—Fun at Google looks different than fun at Patagonia. Just like musical genres, each brand has its own rhythm. And not every company needs costumes and karaoke. Stay on brand. Have fun *your* way. Know your tone and your people, and tailor fun to their personalities and passions. One size doesn't fit all, so mix it up!

- **Measure the vibe**—Survey your team. Track engagement. Listen for signs of burnout or boredom, then remix accordingly.

## FUN-FUELED FAVES

We love household names like Zappos and the Savannah Bananas that are synonymous with infusing fun into their organizational DNA, but I want to share a couple of my lesser-known favorites that truly know how to crank up the fun.

Perhaps not top-of-mind for you (yet), but some of the coolest, most people-focused cultures are being developed in industry-leading companies that are absolutely crushing the "fun" game. These brands are making noise where it counts—inside their own walls. By weaving joy into the everyday, the leaders of these organizations have created environments where people don't just work; they thrive. Check them out.

### FurnitureDealer.Net

In the heart of Minnesota, FurnitureDealer.Net is not just a website development company for furniture brands; it's a powerhouse of employee engagement and innovation. Under the dynamic leadership of CEO Andy Bernstein, the company has carved a niche

# FUN IS EMOTIONAL GLUE FOR ORGANIZATIONS; IT TURNS "WORK FRIENDS" INTO FAMILY.

———

for itself by focusing on its most valuable asset: its people. Bernstein's approach to leadership fosters an environment where fun and productivity go hand in hand. The office buzzes with creative energy, fueled by regular team-building activities, themed office days and spontaneous celebrations. These initiatives make work enjoyable and build a strong sense of camaraderie and loyalty among employees.

The results of this vibrant workplace culture are evident in the company's performance and employee satisfaction. Engaged employees are more motivated and committed, which translates into exceptional service for FurnitureDealer.Net's clients. From hackathons and innovation contests to casual Fridays and office parties, the internal fun initiatives spearheaded by Bernstein have created a thriving, positive work environment. This unique blend of professionalism and playfulness has set FurnitureDealer.Net apart in the industry, driving both employee retention and business growth.

### Carter-Haston

Carter-Haston, a Nashville-based real estate investment company, brings serious play to their workplace culture. Every major team event is a production—from Human Hungry Hippo (yes, the employees are the hippos!) to paper airplane competitions that spark laughter and bonding across departments. I've personally witnessed these fun-filled activities at a Carter-Haston conference. Their events aren't one-offs—they're cultural rituals. It's no surprise they have sky-high employee satisfaction and retention. People feel connected, seen and genuinely excited to show up.

### Beck's Shoes

Beck's Shoes proves you don't need a giant corporate budget to build a culture that kicks—just passion, creativity and a team that's all in. This family-run, purpose-driven powerhouse brings flair to footwear by ditching the stiff corporate vibe and stepping into something way more comfortable: fun. With roots that go back generations and a future focused on people over profits, Beck's creates high-energy work environments where games, competitions and good times are baked into the business model.

One of their signature moves is Wacky Wednesdays— an all-out weekly celebration of absurdity where team members dress up in themed costumes ranging from 80s hair bands to superheroes to "Tourist Dad Chic," competing for prizes and ultimate bragging rights. And these aren't half-hearted efforts—employees go full throttle, turning stores into laugh-filled, customer-engaging hotspots. There are also regular team outings, spontaneous in-store dance-offs and performance contests where top players get hooked up with fantastic rewards. This is how Beck's fuels connection—by making work feel less like a grind and more like a backstage pass to something awesome. It's that kind of buy-in that has created a tight-knit crew with ultra-low turnover and sky-high morale.

Beck's Shoes proves how symbiotic employee engagement and customer experiences are. When the internal beat is strong, the customer experience rocks even harder. Beck's gets it—and they're proof that when you put culture in motion, every step counts. (See what I did there?)

### Sheetz

Family-owned convenience store chain Sheetz doesn't just pump gas—they pump up the vibe. The brand is proof that you can serve up fuel, food and fun, all in the same transaction. It has become synonymous with a joy-filled workplace and over-the-top customer love. At the core? A leadership philosophy that prioritizes people and fun with the same intensity as profits. Think themed employee appreciation days, karaoke contests and even store-versus-store dance battles—yep, all in uniform. Their annual Sheetzfest event is a full-blown celebration where team members are flown in for a weekend of music, awards and culture-building magic. On a daily basis, humorous in-store signage, surprise giveaways and pop-up games bring levity to the fast-paced world of convenience retail. The result? A company where team members stick around and customers keep coming back.

## BarkBox

BarkBox is a dog-obsessed brand that doesn't just talk the talk; they *bark* it out loud and proud through every square inch of their headquarters and beyond. Their offices are a pet paradise, where furry companions are not only welcome—they're full-blown team members. Daily life includes impromptu doggie playdates, treat tastings and, yes, epic canine costume contests that rival any human Halloween party. Staff meetings might be crashed by a Pomeranian in a tutu or a bulldog dressed like Elton John. And nobody bats an eye. Surprise "pawties" break up the routine, and birthday shout-outs often include personalized dog memes or chew-toy bouquets.

This all may sound cute, but it's strategy. BarkBox's silly, irreverent vibe is intentionally baked into the core of their brand, keeping employee morale high and creative energy even higher. The result? A culture that mirrors the same delight customers feel when their pup's monthly box arrives. It's alignment, authenticity and fun, all rolled into one big, wagging culture win.

### Warby Parker

Warby Parker has 20/20 vision when it comes to creating a culture that's as sharp as their eyeglass frames. With a brand built on personality, purpose and a little bit of hipster charm, this industry disruptor is proof that you can be both wildly professional *and* wildly fun. One of their core values is literally "Treat customers the way your grandma would"—and that spirit of kindness and quirk runs through every part of their business.

Inside the office, the company's internal Slack channels double as meme galleries, pet pic showdowns and comedic roasts that would make a stand-up proud. They go *all in* for Halloween—not just casual desk decor or costume headbands but full-on, costume-fueled extravaganzas where entire departments coordinate themes and the CEO shows up in full regalia—face paint, props, the works. They even host annual WarbyCon events, bringing together employees from across the country to connect, create and cut loose—always with a healthy dose of spectacle

# EMPLOYEES WHO FALL MADLY IN LOVE WITH THE EXPERIENCE OF WORKING FOR YOU BECOME FANS FOR LIFE.

———

and storytelling.

Warby Parker's not trying to manufacture fun. They *live* it—infusing humor and heart into every level of the business. That's what makes their culture not only sticky but scalable. It's a reminder that when your people feel empowered to be their authentic, silly selves, productivity doesn't dip—it soars.

## MAKING FUN INTENTIONAL

Fun doesn't mean chaos. It means intentional energy. Structure your fun the same way you plan your strategy: with commitment and alignment. Build rituals that team members look forward to, from weekly themed huddles to surprise pop-ups. Use feedback to evolve the experience. Remember: The goal isn't to distract from work; it's to elevate it.

When you create a place where people can laugh, play and feel fully themselves, you unlock discretionary effort—the kind of magic that can't be bought, only earned. Be the leader that takes fun seriously. Because when your employees fall madly in love with the experience of working for you, they become fans for life. And fans, my friends, are the fuel that will take your culture from garage band to global tour.

## GREATEST HITS

1 **Fun isn't extra, it's essential**—When fun is woven into your cultural DNA (not tacked on as an afterthought), it becomes a powerful catalyst for productivity and engagement.

2 **Joy is your competitive edge**—In a world of burnout, disengagement and quiet quitting, a culture that sparks energy and play is what sets great companies apart.

3 **Make fun intentional**—From daily micro-moments to branded rituals, craft meaningful experiences and traditions that spark fun... with the same intention you apply to your bottom line.

# ENCORE

**W**OW! WE COVERED a *lot* of ground in this book, but the core theme has been the same throughout: A company's culture reaches iconic heights when the brand enhances the overall experience for employees. And that directly affects all external metrics—customer service, brand awareness, sales and profits. In so many ways, those are just the by-products of the concepts we've discussed. Especially since all roads lead back to human behaviors. Take care of the employees and they will essentially take care of everything else, right?

After sharing robust chapters of detailed philosophies, proven statistics and over a hundred legendary brand and leader examples, there should be no doubt that when this is done right, the benefits for your company are monumental. Small businesses and large corporations alike reap huge rewards from a great internal employee culture.

## THE FINAL RECEIPTS

Still, just to give you some final food for thought to validate the importance of employee engagement, a 2023 ITA Group national survey found that job seekers are 15 times more likely to pick a workplace that is "Great Place to Work"–certified—a coveted label every business would love to have. The same survey also found that employees with real work friends are seven times more likely to feel engaged with the brand. The key learning with these two stats is this: When you build a workplace that people genuinely want to come to—where friendships bloom and engagement is embedded—you don't just boost your company's external appeal. You also significantly increase internal loyalty and advocacy.

## NEXT STEPS

So, what now? Well, to keep the fire going in your own quest to amplify your company's employee engagement approach, here are some immediate initiatives you can personally do:

- **Review the "Greatest Hits"**—As a holistic refresher, flip through this book again, paying particular attention to the "Greatest Hits" section at the end of each chapter. Look for opportunities to enhance the company's (or your own) internal employee practices.

- **Share the book**—Distribute copies of *Engagement That Rocks* to your management team, who can be co-catalysts, and collectively discuss how to amp up team member experiences.

- **Get the series**—Read the other books in the "Culture That Rocks" series—*Leadership That Rocks* and *Service That Rocks*—to keep learning about the big focal points of an iconic culture.

- **Pitch external expertise**—You may not be the ultimate decision maker, but recommending new employee engagement material and outside-the-box thinking from an external source is a great way to affect change while also getting you noticed and advancing your career. (And... I happen to know a speaker who can deliver in-person or virtual sessions for this exact strategy.)

Whatever industry you are in, the straightforward but powerful internal practices and stories I have shared will facilitate future growth and immeasurable success for your organization. When building the pillars that will define your organization's employee engagement strategy, your foundation must be anchored to mechanisms that will repeatedly propel people back to your workplace. After all, delivering "engagement that rocks" is a choice that requires intentional focus and consistency. But the work is absolutely worthwhile.

This is how brands become legendary. And sustainable.

I'm so honored that you made *Engagement That Rocks* a part of your journey and a resource in providing clear direction for how you can get team members to fall madly in love with your leadership style and the brand. You now have the power and the opportunity to be the measuring stick for all other companies in your industry. It just takes a little extra attention to engage the team ... and enhance their overall experience.

You got this!

Rock On—

# ACKNOWLEDGMENTS

BIG-TIME THANKS goes to the following family, friends, businesses and mentors who each supported me in some way along the journey to craft *Engagement That Rocks*: my mom (Doris Knight), Stephanie Pilkinton, Bella Rojas, Kathleen Wood, Brian Washburn, Toni Quist, Mike and Carol Shipley, Mike and Tami Kneidinger, Susan Wilson Strom, Melissa Wiggins, Axum Coffee, Rosalie's French Cafe, Just Love Coffee, Foxtail Coffee and the city of Winter Garden, Florida.

My sincerest gratitude goes to Page Two Books, who supported me every step of the way through this adventure—and the entire three-book series—and helped me bring my vision to life. From the first discussion I had with Jesse Finkelstein to the ongoing guidance of the entire team, I always felt I was in great hands.

Huge thank yous go to Kendra Ward and Jenny Govier, my rock star editors at Page Two, who were always a pure joy to work with. Kendra's personality and editorial style embodied the perfect mix of humility and expertise. Jenny's eye for detail and patience helped clarify my professional voice. Together, Kendra and Jenny made me a better writer.

Finally, thank YOU, the reader! I'm seriously blown away that you would take your precious time to read *Engagement That Rocks* and make it a part of your life. Whether it was intended to just be an interesting read to better understand employee engagement or you were on a full-blown quest for a business blueprint to amp up your business, I hope it resonated with you ... and exceeded your expectations. If you get a free moment, reach out and let me know your thoughts. That would be amazing.

# PRODUCTS

## CULTURE THAT ROCKS
**How to Revolutionize a Company's Culture**
2014

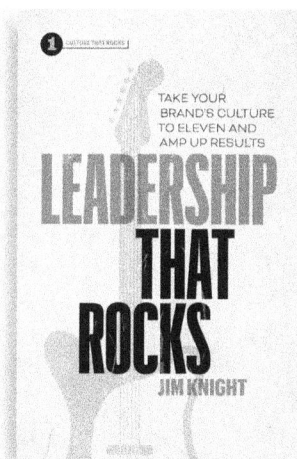

## LEADERSHIP THAT ROCKS
**Take Your Brand's Culture to Eleven and Amp Up Results**
2021

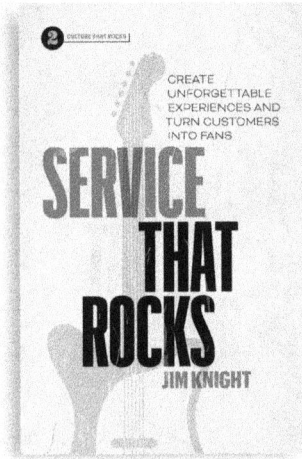

**SERVICE
THAT ROCKS**
Create Unforgettable
Experiences and Turn
Customers into Fans
2022

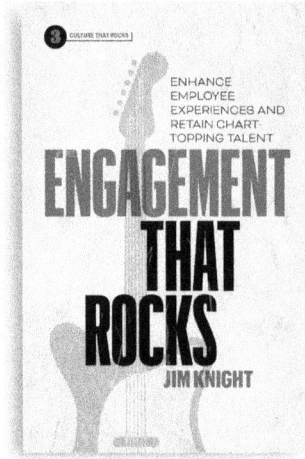

**ENGAGEMENT
THAT ROCKS**
Enhance Employee
Experiences and Retain
Chart-Topping Talent
2026

# ABOUT THE AUTHOR

J IM KNIGHT is an award-winning training and development veteran and culture catalyst who facilitates on a variety of interactive topics, including programs on organizational culture, differentiated service, employee engagement, building rock star teams and leadership.

During Jim's 21-year career with Hard Rock International, his creativity and success garnered his team several industry awards for cutting-edge print, video, e-learning and instructor-led concepts. He was also recognized by *Training* magazine as representing one of the Training Top 125 companies in the world, across all industries, and has since been featured in *Entrepreneur* magazine, *Inc.* magazine, *Forbes* magazine and *Fox Business*. Jim Knight is also a contributing member to *Rolling Stone Magazine*'s Culture Council.

With a music degree in vocal performance and education, a six-year stint as a public middle school teacher and two decades with the Hard Rock brand,

Jim uses all of his experience and expertise—as a keynote speaker, bestselling author and entrepreneur—to assist leaders of all levels and industries in developing their skills and amping up business results.

Jim released his widely praised first book, *Culture That Rocks*, in 2014. It is now in its third edition—and is the impetus for *Engagement That Rocks*, book three in the "Culture That Rocks" series.

To contact Jim Knight, you can reach him at:

**KnightSpeaker.com**

**Jim Knight**

**@JimKnightSpeaker**